MODERN KING'S INDIAN ATTACK

A Complete System for White

by

Senior Master John Hall
Jan R. Cartier

With analytical contributions by Grandmasters

L. Shamkovich, A.Chernin, S. Palatnik

Hays Publishing, *Dallas*

Authors: Senior Master John Hall and Jan R. Cartier
Editor: Lou Hays
Book design and typeset: Lou Hays
Proofreaders: David Sewell, Sid Pickard
Cover chessboard graphic: Joan Meyer

PRINTED IN THE UNITED STATES OF AMERICA

Hays Publishing
P.O. Box 797623
Dallas, Texas 75379

ISBN 1-880673-11-8

CONTENTS

INTRODUCTION

It is with great pleasure that I use this opportunity to congratulate the readers of Jan Cartier's newest work – this time in the field of opening theory – and say a couple of warm words about this book and its co-author, with whom I have had a creative and friendly relationship for over ten years.

The King's Indian Attack began to show up in the repertoire of masters around 1950; this was due mainly to the successes reached by players of the Black pieces in the King's Indian Defense. We can, therefore, understand the willingness of the chessplayers who received satisfaction from the many variations of the King's Indian Defense to have their favorite types of position with the White pieces (and with an "extra" tempo!). The great popularity of these schemes was the basis of Jan's (a thoughtful and delicate chessplayer) idea to write it – to gather and think over the results of the practical use of the King's Indian Attack. The "extra" tempo of the King's Indian Attack gives rise to interesting new vistas of opening theory. Black must be careful when faced with this dynamic and modern system; this is especially the case if Black undertakes to play the way White would play against the King's Indian Defense.

Jan Cartier and his co-author, Senior Master John Hall, with exacting and innovative analyses, have brought out for both sides, a new and deep field of recommendations on how to play this refined opening system – we thank them for that.

S. Palatnik
International Grandmaster

THE KING'S INDIAN ATTACK
Special Edition
by Leonid Shamkovich, International Grandmaster

The King's Indian Attack (KIA), is a reversed form of the King's Indian Defense. The typical plan of development is based on the moves Nf3, g3, Bg2, Nbd2 and e4 – established by various possible move orders. Black usually doesn't copy White's active plans (used against the King's Indian Defense), preferring more restrained strategies. Otherwise, with the intrinsic extra tempo of the KIA, White has chances for a serious initiative. Therefore we should recognize the KIA as an independent strategical opening, with original theory and practice.

The really classic games for the modern interpretation of the KIA are seen in the efforts of Botvinnik, L.Stein and Bobby Fischer, whose great expertise lay the foundations of contemporary KIA theory.

One of White's main strategical ideas in the KIA is a step by step preparation for a strong attack on the Kingside. The classic method for this action is the central advance e4-e5, with a following concentration of forces against the Black King.

Typical positions of the KIA can appear, as we shall see, after the first moves of different openings such as the Sicilian, French, Caro-Kann, Reti and Alekhine Defense.

M.Botvinnik-W.Uhlmann, Alekhine Memorial, Moscow 1956, French Defense/KIA **1.e4 e6 2.d3 d5 3.Nd2 Nf6 4.Ngf3 c5 5.g3 Nc6 6.Bg2 Be7 7.0-0 0-0 8.Re1 Rb8 9.e5 Nd7 10.Nf1 b5** (The best chance for an effective counterattack) **11.h4 Ba6?** (11...b4!?) **12.N1h2 b4 13.Bf4 Bb5 14.Bh3 c4?** (14...a5!?) **15.d4** (+=) **15...Qb6 16.Be3 Rfc8 17.Ng5** (With the threat 18.Nxe6) **17...Nf8 18.f4 Nd8 19.f5** (19.g4!? – Botvinnik) **19...exf5 20.Bxf5 Nde6 21.Qf3 Nxg5** (21...Nxd4? 22.Qf2) **22.hxg5 Rd8 23.Ng4!** (White's Knight rushes to f6) **23...Ng6?** (23...Bd7!?) **24.Kg2 Bd7** (Too late) **25.Bxd7 Rxd7 26.Rh1** (White has fulfilled his general program and now goes over to a decisive offensive) **26...Qe6 27.Rh5! Rb6 28.Rah1 Nf8 29.Nf6+!**

29...gxf6 30.gxf6 Bxf6 31.exf6 Qe4 (Going into an ending will not save Black) **32.Qxe4 dxe4 33.Rg5+ Ng6 34.Rc5 Rxf6 35.Rc8+ Nf8 36.Rh4!** and White won in a few moves.

L.Stein-A.Sokolsky, Odessa 1960, Reti/KIA **1.Nf3 d5 2.g3 Nf6 3.Bg2 g6 4.0-0 Bg7 5.d3 0-0 6.Nbd2 c5 7.e4 e6** (Botvinnik-Donner, Leiden 1970, continued 7...Nc6 8.c3 b6 9.Re1 [9.e5!? Ng4 10.d4 cxd4 11.cxd4 Ba6 12.Re1 Nb4? 13.h3! Nh6 14.Qa4! winning] 9...dxe4 10.dxe4 Ng4 11.e5! +=; but 10...e5 is possible) **8.Re1 Nc6 9.c3 b6?!** (9...dxe4!?) **10.e5! Nd7 11.d4 f6?!** (This attempt to challenge White's center leads to a weakening of the e5-square; better was 11...cxd4 12.cxd4 Ba6) **12.exf6 Qxf6 13.Nb3 Ba6 14.Be3 Bc4 15.dxc5 Bxb3 16.axb3 Nxc5 17.Ng5 Rfe8 18.b4 Nb7 19.Bxd5! Rad8** (After 19...exd5 20.Qxd5+ Kh8 21.Nf7+ Kg8 22.Nh6+ Kh8 23.Bg5! is crushing) **20.Bxc6!** (A brilliant Queen sacrifice) **20...Rxd1 21.Rexd1 Rb8 22.Rxa7** (White has more than enough compensation for the Queen) **22...Nd8 23.Bg2 h6 24.Ne4 Qf5 25.R1d7 Be5 26.Bxh6 Nc6**

27.Rg7+!! (A spectacular thrust: now two minor pieces are stronger than the Black Queen) **27...Bxg7 28.Rxg7+ Kh8 29.Rc7! Qe5 30.Bf4 Qf5 31.Rxc6** and White won.

L.Stein-I.Birbrager, USSR Team Championship, Moscow 1966 Caro-Kann/KIA **1.e4 c6 2.d3 d5 3.Nd2 dxe4** (3...g6!?) **4.dxe4 Nf6 5.Ngf3 Bg4 6.h3 Bh5?** (6...Bxf3!?) **7.e5 Nd5 8.e6!** (The classical "blockading" sacrifice. The e6-pawn completely stifles Black's development) **8...f6 9.g4 Bg6 10.Nd4 Nc7 11.c3 Qd5 12.Qb3! Qxh1 13.Qxb7 Kd8 14.N2f3** (Now Black's Queen is shut out of play) **14...Bd3 15.Bf4! Qxf1+ 16.Kd2 Qxf2+ 17.Kxd3 Nxe6** (17...Nba6 18.Kc4! and mate is inevitable) **18.Nxe6+ Ke8 19.Qc8+ Kf7 20.Ng5+** and Black Resigned; if 20...Kg6 then 21.Qe8+ Kh6 22.Qh5#; or 20...fxg5 21.Nxg5+ Kf6 22.Qe6#.

Jakov Yuchtman from Odessa, who died in New York in 1985, was another great admirer and specialist in the KIA. Here is one of his best games:

Yuchtman-Zilberman, Odessa 1968, French/KIA **1.e4 e6 2.d3 c5 3.g3 Nc6 4.Bg2 d6 5.Nf3 Nf6 6.0-0 Be7 7.Nbd2 0-0 8.Re1 Bd7 9.a4 Qc7 10.Nc4 Rfd8 11.a5 Ne8 12.Bf4** (+=; the goal is e4-e5) **12...b5 13.axb6 e.p. axb6 14.Rxa8 Rxa8 15.e5 d5 16.Ne3 Qd8 17.h4 Nd4 18.Ng5! h6**

19.Nxf7!!

(A sacrifice to destroy the Black Kingside fortress) **19...Kxf7 20.c3 Nc6 21.Qh5+ Kg8 22.Nxd5!** (Another powerful sac) **22...Nc7** (22...exd5 23.Bxd5+ Kh8 24.Bxh6 winning) **23.Nxc7 Qxc7 24.Qg6 Bf8 25.Be4** (White's attack cannot be stopped) **25...Ra4 26.Qh7+ Kf7 27.Bg6+ Ke7 28.Bxh6 Nxe5 29.Bxg7! Nf3+ 30.Kf1!** (30.Kh1?? Rxh4+ and Black wins) **30...Kd8 31.Qh8! Qd6 32.Bxf8 Nh2+ 33.Ke2 Re4+?** (33...Qd5 34.Bd6+ wins) **34.Bxe4** and Black Resigned.

Bobby Fischer used to play the KIA with White in the early years of his career, and very successfully. But he never tried it in the Candidates or World Championship Matches. Let us consider one of his best early efforts.

Fischer-Sherwin, New Jersey Open 1957, Sicilian/KIA **1.e4 c5 2.Nf3 e6 3.d3 Nc6 4.g3 Nf6 5.Bg2 Be7 6.O-O O-O 7.Nbd2 Rb8 8.Re1 d6 9.c3 b6 10.d4 Qc7?** (10...cxd4 11.cxd4 d5 12.e5 Ne8 13.Nf1 Ba6 +=) **11.e5! Nd5 12.exd6 Bxd6 13.Ne4 c4 14.Nxd6 Qxd6 15.Ng5! Nce7 16.Qc2 Ng6 17.h4 Nf6** (17...h6 18.h5! wins)

18.Nxh7! Nxh7 (18...Kxh7 19.Bf4! wins) **19.h5 Nh4 20.Bf4 Qd8 21.gxh4 Rb7! 22.h6!** (22.Bxb7? Bxb7 with counterattack – the threat would be 23...Qd5) **22...Qxh4 23.hxg7 Kxg7?** (23...Rd8!? +=; now White's attack is decisive) **24.Re4! Qh5 25.Re3! f5 26.Rh3 Qe8 27.Be5+ Nf6 28.Qd2 Kf7 29.Qg5 Qe7 30.Bxf6** (30.Rh6!?) **30...Qxf6 31.Rh7+ Ke8 32.Qxf6 Rxh7 33.Bc6+** and Black Resigned.

ACKNOWLEDGEMENTS

The authors wish to give thanks to Grandmasters Shamkovich and Palatnik for their important contributions to this book. We are especially indebted to Grandmaster Alexander Chemin for his marvelous and instructive section on Bobby Fischer's treatment of the KIA in French setups (Chapter 4). Special thanks to my good friend and co-author, Jan R. Cartier (in charge of financial services in his position as Executive Vice-President of Ryan, Beck Planning and Insurance Services, Inc.) whose remarkable talents in chess, business and the artistic realms have been indispensible to this as well as other chess projects. We gratefully acknowledge the encouragement and valued assistance of the other members of the staff at Ryan, Beck.

**John Hall
USCF Senior Master**

The authors wish to give a special acknowledgement and thanks to Joan Meyer for the most unusual and intriguing chessboard created for the front cover of this book.

Joan was born in Long Island and spent her childhood in upstate New York. She attended Tyler School of Art and received a fellowship to the North Carolina School of the Arts, majoring in Theatre Set Design and Scene Painting.

After moving to Florida, Joan received a Masters Degree from Florida Atlantic University and was subsequently represented by the Joy Moos and Barbara Gilman Galleries. She was also deeply involved in the art scene with "Artifacts," a group which sets the tone for all of the groundbreaking and on Edge Art at events, clubs and galleries in Miami and South Florida.

Joan's works, which are very identifiable through her original and unusual visual vocabulary, have won numerous major awards.

In 1989, she moved to New York City to further pursue her art career. She supports her work by teaching in the New York City school system and currently resides in Soho, New York.

Finally, a word of thanks to my co-author, John Hall. I have enjoyed his works for many years, and I have immense respect for his writing and chess playing abilities.

Jan R.Cartier

CHAPTER ONE

THE KIA vs. SICILIAN SYSTEM
(with ...g6 and ...Bg7; ...e6 [or ...e5] and ...Nge7)

Game 1
Hunerfauth-Winz
Correspondence 1989/91

1.e4 e6 (When World Champion Kasparov plays this system as Black he plays 1...c5 and after 2.Nf3 e6 [ready to unleash his favorite Scheveningen Variation after 3.d4 cxd4 4.Nxd4 Nf6 5.Nc3 d6] 3.d3, play will transpose into the opening moves of this chapter – e.g., see Game 9) **2.d3 d5 3.Nd2 c5 4.Ngf3 Nc6 5.g3 Nge7 6 Bg2 g6 7.0-0 Bg7 8.Qe2!?** (A promising alternative to the standard 8.Re1) **8...0-0** (Early Kingside castling by Black in this Sicilian System is often ill-advised. Usually this is because White can then push e4-e5, cramping Black's center and Kingside, thus creating proper strategical preconditions for a steady increase of pressure there [see Games 3 and 4 for an illustration of White's chances in this type of scenario]. Here Black, doubtless aware of this potentiality, has in mind a sharp rejoinder to undermine White's "right" to attack on the Kingside) **9.c3 b6 10.Re1** (Note that White might have transposed into this position via 8.Re1 with a later 10.Qe2) **10...Ba6 11.e5** (This thematic thrust of the e-pawn creates a charged situation) **11...g5?!**

(see next diagram)

(This is the counterstroke alluded to in the note to Black's 8th. The idea of 11...g5 is to destroy White's vital e5-pawn. However, in this particular position it fails; but, as we shall see in several other games in this section, the move ...g5 must be watched closely, as it can be very effective in some cases) **12.Nxg5!** (Not 12.h3? Ng6) **12...Nxe5 13.Qh5 Bxd3** (Now

After 11...g5?!

Black must have felt happy with his game, as he has blasted away White's center and seems to have plenty of pieces to defend his Kingside; then his central control should give him an excellent game) **14.Rxe5!!** (But this tremendous tactical shot refutes Black's strategical dreams) **14...h6** (Forced. After 14...Bxe5 15.Be4!! Bxe4 16.Nxe4 Black's h7 is disastrously weak) **15.Ngf3 Qd6?!** (Leaving Black with only one pawn for the piece, but hoping to create a massive pawn center as compensation. But a piece is a piece! Yet even after the better line 15...Bg6 16.Qh3 Bxe5 17.Nxe5 Kg7 18.Ndf3 Rh8 19.Nh4 Black is in bad shape) **16.Re1 Bg6 17.Qh4 e5 18.Qa4 f5 19.Nh4 f4 20.Nxg6 Nxg6 21.Qb3! Rad8 22.c4 d4** (Now with Black's center pawns blockaded, the rest is a matter of technique) **23.Ne4 Qd7 24.a4 Qg4 25.f3 Qh5 26.g4 Qh4 27.Bd2 Qe7 28.a5 Rb8 29.axb6 Rxb6 30.Qa3 Rfb8 31.Qxc5 Qxc5 32.Nxc5 Rxb2 33.Ne4 Rc2 34.Rec1 Rxc1** (Black displays an awesome will to survive— but little else) **35.Rxc1 Ne7 36.c5 Nc6 37.Bf1 Kf8 38.Bc4 Ke8 39.Bd5 Kd7 40.Ra1 Bf8 41.Ra6 Rc8 42.Bxc6+** (This wins, but more incisive was 42.Nf6+ Ke7 43.Bxc6 since 43...Kxf6 loses to 44.Bb7+) **42...Rxc6 43.Rxc6 Kxc6 44.h4 Kb5 45.g5 hxg5 46.hxg5 a5 47.Kf2 Bg7 48.Ke2 Bf8 49.Kd3 Bg7 50.Bc1 Bf8 51.Ba3 Bg7 52.g6 Black Resigns.**

Game 2
Maljutin-Magerramov
Moscow 1991

1.e4 c5 2.Nf3 e6 3.d3 Nc6 4.g3 g6 5.Bg2 Bg7 6.0-0 Nge7 7.c3 d5
8.Qe2 (White uses the same deployment for the Queen as in Game 1.
However, note that the usual Nbd2 has been omitted; this allows the QN
to have creative options for its development) 8...h6 (Feinting at a possible
...g5, which White promptly restrains) 9.h4 b6 (Black avoids early
Kingside castling to keep from giving White a definite target for attack)
10.e5 Qc7 11.Re1 Ba6 12.a4! (Now we see why White has left the QN
at home; it will head for a fine post on b5 via a3) 12...Rd8 (If 12...Na5
then 13.Nbd2 and the Na5 is poorly placed, while Rb1 and b4 looms)
13.Na3 0-0 14.Nb5 Qd7 15.Bf4 Nf5 16.Bh3 Bb7 17.Bxf5!

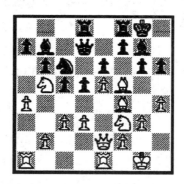

(A surprising but insightful exchange. Now if 17...gxf5 then 18.d4 and
Black's Kingside is vulnerable and the Bb7 is locked out of play; so the
"weakening" of White's light squares is inconsequential) 17...exf5
(Avoiding the weakening of the Kingside, but now White breaks through
on the e-file) 18.e6 fxe6 (On 18...Qe7 19.Qd2! is strong) 19.Qxe6+ Qxe6
20.Rxe6 d4 (On 20...Kf7 simply 21.Rae1 is powerful, so Black tries to
stir up some activity by opening the diagonal for the "sleeping" QB)
21.cxd4 Rf6 22.Rae1 Nb4 23.Re8+ Rxe8+ 24.Rxe8+ Kf7 25.Re3 Nc2
26.Ne5+ (Not 26.Nd6+? Rxd6) 26...Kg8 27.Re2 Nxd4 28.Nxd4 cxd4

29.Nd7 Rc6 (On 29...Rf7 30.Re8+ Kh7 31.Ne5 is strong) 30.Re7 Rc2 31.Bxh6! (A nice shot, winning material) 31...Bxh6 32.Nf6+ Kf8 33.Rxb7 Bd2 34.Nd7+ Kg8 35.Nf6+ Kf8 36.Nd7+ Kg8 37.Rxa7 Be1 38.Nxb6 Bxf2+ 39.Kg2 Be3+ 40.Kh3 (Not 40.Kf3?? Rf2#) 40...Bg1 41.g4 f4 42.g5 (The rest of the game is a matter of brilliant technique) 42...f3 43.Ra8+ Kg7 44.Ra7+ Kg8 45.Ra8+ Kg7 46.Nc4 Be3 47.Ra7+ Kg8 48.Ra6! f2 49.Rxg6+ Kh7 50.Rf6 Rc1 51.a5! f1=Q+ 52.Rxf1 Rxf1 53.a6 Ra1 54.Na3 Rc1 55.a7 Rc8 56.Nb5! Ra8 57.Kg4 Bd2 58.Kf5 Ba5 59.Kf6 Kg8 60.h5 Bb6 61.h6 Bxa7 62.Nc7 Rf8+ 63.Kg6 Rf3 64.Nd5 Rxd3 65.Nf6+ Kf8 66.Kh7! Rg3 67.g6 d3 68.g7+ Kf7 69.Ne4 Rg2 70.Nd6+ Ke6 71.Nc4 Kf7 72.Ne5+ Ke6 73.Ng6 **Black Resigns.**

Game 3
Dvoretzky-Ubilava
U.S.S.R. 1979

1.e4 c5 2.Nf3 e6 3.d3 d5 4.Nbd2 Nc6 5.g3 g6 6.Bg2 Bg7 7.0-0 Nge7 8.Re1 0-0 (As mentioned in Game 1, early castling Kingside in this Sicilian System is often fraught with danger. Very slight differences in the position can be of major significance. White's next move is a strictly thematic, but [in this exact position], premature thrust of the e-pawn) 9.e5?! (This is not the right moment for this key pawn push. Correct is 9.h4 [preventing ...g5], or 9.Qe2!?, as in Game 1) 9...Qc7 10.Qe2 a5? (Black is not aware of his opportunity to strike back effectively with 10...g5!, which knocks out the props of the advanced e-pawn. No doubt he overlooked this move because it seems to grossly violate the age-old tenet that "wild" pawn advances in front of the castled King position are suicidal. But there are exceptions to the general rule, as this game could have shown if Ubilava had looked more closely at the particulars of the position. After 10...g5! play could have proceeded 11.Nxg5 [after 11.h3 Ng6 12.Nb3 h6 13.Nxc5 Ncxe5 we prefer Black, mainly because of his central pawn superiority] 11...Qxe5 12.Qxe5 Nxe5 13.Nf1 Nf5 and in the game Damljanovic-Georgadze, Belgrade 1992, White meekly acquiesced to a draw here) **11.h4!** (Now everything is back on track for White. The rest of this game is a fine illustration of the thematic details of a well-conducted KIA Kingside attack with the forward pawn on e5) **11...h6 12.Nf1** (Now ...g5 is permanently out of the question. Also, from f1 this Knight can circulate into effective play via h2-g4 [or sometimes e3-g4] with increasing piece pressure against Black's center and Kingside) **12...a4 13.a3** (Preventing 13...a3, which would punch holes in White's Queenside pawn structure) **13...b5?!** (Better was 13...Nd4!?. Black must seek the most active counterplay in such positions or be crushed on the Kingside) **14.N1h2 b4 15.Bf4 Kh7 16.Ng4**

(White's pieces form a most impressive alignment against Black's center and Kingside. The five-fold "overprotection" of e5 would have gladdened Nimzowitch's heart!) **16...Ng8 17.c4!** (A very well conceived move. White wants to threaten to play h5, answering ...g5 with Bxg5; but this finesseful move induces Black to eventually weaken e4 – see Black's 19th move – and the use of the e4 square will strongly enhance White's follow up to the sacrifice on g5) **17...bxc3 e.p. 18.bxc3 Ba6 19.c4!** (Back again! Now the threat of 20.cxd5 exd5 21.e6 induces Black to trade pawns, but this gives White the central e4 square) **19...dxc4 20.dxc4 Rab8 21.h5!** (The tempting 20.Nf6+ can be answered by

20...Kh8) **21...Kh8** (After 21...g5 22.Bxg5 hxg5 23.Nxg5+ Kh8 24.Bxc6 Qxc6 25.Qd3 is curtains, or 24...f5 25.exf6 e.p. Nxf6 26. Qc2! and Black can resign) **22.hxg6 fxg6 23.Nf6! Nge7 24.Rad1 Rbd8 25.Rd6!** (Note the piquant invasion on the dark squares d6 and f6 – made possible by the starring role of the e5-pawn) **25...Bb7** (25...Bxf6 26.exf6 Rxd6 27.fxe7 Qxe7 28.Ne5!) **26.Rxe6 Nd4 27.Nxd4 cxd4 28.Qd3 Bxg2 29.Kxg2 Rf7 30.Rh1** (All of White's pieces close in on the hapless Black King) **30...Nf5 31.g4 Qb7+ 32.Kg1 Ne3** (Sheer desperation) **33.Bxe3 Qf3 34.Qxg6 Bxf6 35.Rxh6+ Black Resigns.**

Game 4
Dvoretsky-Khalifman
Sverdlovsk 1987

1.e4 c5 2.Nf3 e6 3.d3 d5 4.Nbd2 Nc6 5.g3 g6 6.Bg2 Bg7 7.0-0 Nge7 8.Re1 0-0 (As mentioned in notes to previous games, this early castling can be dangerous for Black) **9.e5?!** (The same error seen in Game 3 where we saw that 9...Qc7 10.Qe2 g5! is fine for Black. We give this game despite these early inaccuracies since the later play is very instructive) **9...Qc7 10.Qe2 b6?!** (10...g5!) **11.h4!** (Stopping ...g5) **11...Ba6 12.Nf1 Nd4** (The idea is to play on the c-file after the exchange on d4) **13.Nxd4 cxd4 14.Bf4 Nc6?!** (Dubious, as it blocks play on the c-file. Better was Dvoretsky's recommendation 14...Rac8 15.Rac1 Qc5 though after 16.Nh2 followed by Ng4 and h5 White has good chances on the Kingside) **15.a3 Qd7** (On 15...Rac8 Dvoretsky notes that White should play 16.Rac1! as the direct 16.Nh2 allows the troublesome response 16...Bxe5! 17.Bxe5 Qxe5 18.Qxe5 Nxe5 19.Rxe5 Rxc2. With 15...Qd7 Black is maneuvering to get in ...f6) **16.Nh2 Rae8 17.Ng4 f6**

(see next diagram)

(After 17...h5 Dvoretsky gives 18.Nf6+ Bxf6 19.exf6 [threat: 20.Bh6] 19...Kh7 20.Be5! followed by f4 with a crushing bind, as Black is

After 17...f6

helpless against a breakthrough by g3-g4. The text tries to head off
White's attack, but the surrender of the dark-squared Bishop is like
throwing gas on a fire) **18.exf6 Bxf6 19.Nxf6+ Rxf6 20.Bh3 Rxf4** (A
rather desperate sac, but it is hard to find anything good for Black here
as on 20...Bc8 21.Be5 is powerful) **21.gxf4 Bc8 22.Qf3** (Not 22.f5 e5!)
22...Qf7 23.Qg3 Kh8 (On 23...Rf8 24.f5!) **24.Re2 Rf8 25.Rae1 Nd8
26.f5!** (Forcing a won ending) **26...gxf5** (26...exf5 27.Re7) **27.Qe5+
Qg7+** (27...Kg8? 28.f4 and Rg2+) **28.Qxg7+ Kxg7 29.f4 Kf6 30.Rg2
Bd7 31.Kf2 Nf7 32.Ke2** (Better was 32.Reg1 Rc8 33.Ke1 Nh8 34.h5
and Rg8. Dvoretsky) **32...Nh8! 33.Rf1 Ng6 34.h5 Ne7 35.h6 Ng6
36.Kd2 Rc8 37.Rg3 Be8 38.Rf2 Bf7 39.Bf1 Rc7 40.Be2 Rc8 41.Rg1
Ke7 42.Bh5 Kd6 43.c3 dxc3+ 44.bxc3 Ke7 45.Bxg6 Bxg6 46.a4!** (To
open lines for his Rooks) **46...Kd6 47.Rb1 Kc5 48.Rb5+ Kc6 49.Ke3
Kd6 50.Kd4 Rg8 51.Rg2 Black Resigns.**

Game 5
Bologan-Lautier
Chalkidiki 1992

   **1.e4 c5 2.Nf3 e6 3.d3 Nc6 4.g3 d5 5.Nbd2 g6 6.Bg2 Nge7 7.0-0 Bg7
8.Re1 0-0 9.h4** (Not 9.e5?! Qc7 10.Qe2 g5! – see Games 1, 3 and 4)
9...h6 (Black must be prepared to meet h5 with ...g5) **10.e5 f5?!** (Very
aggressive, but we feel this is not objectively good. Black can't weaken

his pawns while "demanding" the initiative against the fundamentally sound KIA structure! Also, if 10...Qc7 then 11.Qe2 and now 11...g5? fails as 12.hxg5 hxg5 13.Nxg5 Qxe5 14.Nde4!! dxe4 15.Qh5 wins. Oratovski) **11.exf6 e.p. Rxf6 12.Nh2!?** (Quite playable, but we like 12.Nf1! [our exclamation] when Lautier intended 12...Qd6! [his exclamation] followed by 13...e5. But we give 12.Nf1! Qd6 13.Ne3! e5 14.c4 with advantage to White. Black's center has been formed too precipitously and is a juicy target for White's well-coordinated forces) **12...Rf7 13.Ng4 Qd6 14.Nf3?**

(Overlooking a tactical point. Correct was 14.Nb3!? – see Game 18) **14...e5! 15.Ne3** (Clearly White overlooked that after 15.Nxh6+ Bxh6 16.Bxh6 Bg4! the pin will win material) **15...Be6** (Now Black's massive center and big lead in development give him a terrific initiative) **16.c4** (Too little, too late) **16...Raf8** (Threat: 17...d4 and 18...Bg4) **17.Nd2 Rxf2! 18.cxd5 Rxg2+** (A fine sac of the Exchange maintains a strong attack) **19.Kxg2 Nxd5 20.Ne4 Qe7 21.Bd2?** (The only try was 21.Nxd5 to prevent the following sacrifice) **21...Nf4+! 22.gxf4 exf4 23.Nf1** (Not 23.Ng4 f3+) **23...Qxh4** (Threat: 24...f3+) **24.Nh2** (24.Qf3 is mashed by 24...Nd4) **24...f3+ 25.Qxf3** (Or 25.Nxf3 Qh3+ 26.Kf2 Qh2+ 27.Ke3 Bd4+ 28.Nxd4 cxd4#) **25...Rxf3 26.Nxf3 Qh3+ 27.Kf2 Nd4 28.Nxd4 Bxd4+ 29.Be3 Bg4! 30.Bxd4 Qf3+ 31.Kg1 Bh3 White Resigns.**

Game 6
Damljanovic-Lautier
Pamplona 1992/93

1.Nf3 c5 2.e4 e6 3.d3 d5 4.Nbd2 Nc6 5.g3 g6 6.Bg2 Bg7 7.0-0 Nge7 8.Re1 b6 (This is the treatment preferred by many top players today. Black delays Kingside castling while setting up conditions for counterplay on the Queenside and center, as the occasion may demand) **9.c3** (Blocking the action of the Bg7 and allowing possibilities of a later e5 followed by d4, or even a3 and b4. However, Dolmatov believes that 9.Nf1 is the best continuation for White. See note to White's 10th. But best of all seems to be the sharp 9.exd5! – see Game 11) **9...a5** (A key move in this pattern; Black gains Queenside space [...a4 is a further possibility] while allowing the QR to shuffle into play via a7) **10.a4** (Stopping 10...a4. Interesting is 10.Nf1!? to which the best reply is 10...d4 or even 10...a4. For the reply 10...dxe4?! see Game 8) **10...Ra7** (In the game Benjamin-Eingorn, St. John 1988, Black eschewed the ...Ra7 maneuver in favor of ...Ba6; this favored White – see Game 10) **11.h4 h6 12.exd5** (For the move 12.Nb3!? see Game 9) **12...exd5** (After 12...Nxd5 White has c4 as an outpost for the QN) **13.Nb3** (Preparing to strike with d4, which would fix Black's d-pawn as a strategic pressure point, hence Black's reply) **13...d4 14.cxd4 cxd4 15.Bf4 0-0 16.Ne5 Nxe5 17.Bxe5**

(see next diagram)

17...Bb7! (Best. In Yudasin-M.Vukic, Bern 1989, Black played the inaccurate 17...Bxe5? and after 18.Rxe5 Qd6 19.Qe2 Be6 20.Nd2 Nc6 White found the powerful Exchange sac 21.Rxe6! fxe6 [21...Qxe6 22.Qxe6 fxe6 23.Bxc6] 22.Nc4 Qd7 23.Nxb6 Qe8 24.Rc1 with a winning position) **18.Bxb7 Rxb7 19.Rc1 Nf5 20.Qf3** (Attacking the Rook while stopping the centralizing ...Qd5) **20...Re7 21.Bxg7 Kxg7** (The position has become drawish – no pawn majorities and both sides have

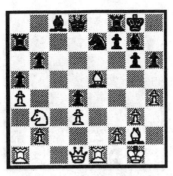

After 17.Bxe5

the same type of pieces – i.e., no Bishop vs. Knight imbalances) **22.Nd2 Rxe1+ 23.Rxe1 Re8 24.Rc1 Re6 25.Qf4 Qd5 26.Ne4 Qb3** (Raiding the Queenside pawns, but White meanwhile eyes the somewhat vulnerable Black Kingside) **27.Qf3 Qxa4 28.Rc7 Rc6 29.Qf4 Rxc7 30.Qe5+ Kf8 31.Qxc7 Qd1+ 32.Kh2 Qxd3 33.Qd8+ Kg7 34.Qf6+ Kg8 35.Qd8+ Kg7 36.Qf6+ Kg8 37.Qd8+ Draw.**

Game 7
Dvoretsky-Vulfson
U.S.S.R. 1986

1.e4 c5 2.Nf3 e6 3.d3 Nc6 4.g3 d5 5.Nbd2 g6 6.Bg2 Bg7 7.0-0 Nge7 8.exd5! (A theoretical novelty of great importance. White exchanges in order to follow up with a deep pawn sacrifice) **8...exd5** (After 8...Nxd5 9.Nb3 b6 10.c4 Nde7 11.d4 cxd4 12.Nfxd4 Bb7 13.Bg5 White has an initiative)

(see next diagram)

9.d4!! (A move of great strategic and tactical depth. The ideas are to exploit Black's lagging development and to target Black's d-pawns) **9...cxd4** (After 9...c4 10.c3 the Black d-pawn will be permanently fixed and thereby subject to increasing pressure from White's pieces. The text aims to retain the extra pawn, but White shows some sparkling tactics to gain the initiative) **10.Nb3 Qb6?!** (After 10...Bg4 11.h3 Bxf3 12.Qxf3

After 8...exd5

0-0 13.Bf4, then Rfe1 and Rad1 White has good positional compensation
for the pawn –Dvoretsky. Nonetheless, this was likely Black's best line)
11.Bg5 (Dvoretsky gives 11.Bf4! 0-0 12.Bd6 and Bc5 as stronger. Many
of the following notes are derived from Dvoretsky) **11...Nf5?!** (Better
11...0-0! 12.Nfxd4 Nf5 with equal play) **12.Re1+ Be6 13.g4!** (White
plays sharply to exploit Black's uncastled King) **13...Nd6 14.Nfxd4!
Bxd4** (14...Nxd4 15.Be3 N6b5 16.a4!) **15.Nxd4 Qxd4** (15...Nxd4
16.Bf6 0-0 17.Bxd4 keeps White on top) **16.Bxd5!** (Accurate. Not
16.Qxd4? Nxd4 17.Bf6 Nxc2 with Black winning) **16...0-0!** (If
16...Qxd1 17.Raxd1 Nb5 [17...Kd7 18.Bf4!] 18.Bf6 and now 18...0-0
19.Rxe6! fxe6 20.Bxe6+ Rf7 21.Rd7 Raf8 22.c3, or 18...Rf8 19.Re3!
threatening 20.Bxc6+ bxc6 21.Red3. This game, among others, will
certainly dispel the erroneous notion that the KIA is devoid of interesting
tactical play!) **17.Bxc6 Qc5!** (Black defends deftly. Poor was 17...Qxd1
18.Raxd1 bxc6 19.Rxd6 Bxg4 20.Rxc6 – the opposite colored Bishops
do not offset the extra pawn; or, 17...Qxg4+ 18.Qxg4 Bxg4 19.Bg2 and
the two Bishops combined with the Queenside pawn majority give a clear
advantage) **18.Bf3!** (The only way to maintain the pressure. After 18.Bd5
Qxd5! [18...Bxd5? 19.Re5! Ne4 20.Be3] 19.Qxd5 Bxd5 20.Rad1 Bf3
21.Rxd6 Bxg4 the opposite colored Bishops with even material should
draw. Or if 18.Be7 Qxc6 19.Qxd6 Qxd6 20.Bxd6 Rfd8 recovers the pawn
with even chances) **18...Qxg5 19.Qxd6 Rac8 20.c3 Qb5!** (Not

20...Bxg4? 21.Qg3! h5 22.h3. On 20...h5 21.h3 hxg4 22.hxg4 Bxg4 23.Qg3 f5 [23...Rc4 24.Bxb7] either Re5 or Re6 favors White) **21.Rad1 Bxa2** (Not 21...Qxb2? 22.Rxe6! fxe6 23.Qxe6+ Kg7 24.Rd7+ Kh6 25.Qe3+ g5 26.Qe6+ mating) **22.Rd2 Rfd8** (After 22...Rfe8 23.Re7 Rxe7 24.Qxe7 Re8 25.Qxb7 Re1+ 26.Kg2 Qf1+ 27.Kg3, or 22...Be6 23.Re5! White stays on top) **23.Qxd8+ Rxd8 24.Rxd8+ Kg7 25.Rd2** (The two Rooks are stronger than Black's Queen, but it is difficult to make decisive progress) **25...h5 26.h3 Be6 27.Re4 a5 28.Red4 hxg4 29.hxg4 Qg5 30.Kg2 b6 31.Re2 Qc5 32.Kg3 Qb5 33.Rdd2 Qg5 34.Re3 Qc5 35.Be2 Qc6?! 36.f3?!** (Missing 36. f4! with an important gain of space [f4-f5 or g4-g5 are possible] and some real winning chances) **36...g5!** (Exploiting White's omission. Now its a dead draw) **37.Rd4 Qc7+ 38.Kg2 Kf6 39.Bd3 Qc5 40.Be4 Qb5 41.Rd2 Qe5 42.Ree2 Qb5 43.Bb7 Qc5 44.Rd4 b5 45.Red2 Ke5 Draw.**

Game 8
Dolmatov-A. Sokolov
Manila Interzonal 1990

    1.e4 e6 2.d3 d5 3.Nd2 c5 4.Ngf3 Nc6 5.g3 g6 6.Bg2 Bg7 7.0-0 Nge7 8.Re1 b6 9.c3 (Dolmatov thinks 9.Nf1 is best; the endgame after 9...dxe4 10.dxe4 Qxd1 11.Rxd1 slightly favors White. This game is a good illustration of the nagging pull White usually has in such endings. For 9.exd5! see Game 11) **9...a5 10.Nf1** (The "usual" 10.a4 is less good after White has played c3, since after 10.a4 d4 11.c4 a glaring hole appears on b4) **10...dxe4** (Challenging White to make something of the endgame, which he does. We like 10...d4 or even 10...a4 as better choices) **11.dxe4 Qxd1 12.Rxd1 a4** (Trying to constrict White's Queenside while stopping 13.a4 – which would nail down control of b5 and c4; this is probably why Black was content to enter this ending. But Dolmatov reveals some subtle resources for White to retain an edge) **13.Rb1!**

(This sneaky Rook move prevents 13...a3 as then 14.bxa3 would attack Black's b6-pawn) **13...0-0 14.Bf4 e5** (After 14...a3 15.Rdc1! axb2 16.Rxb2 the b6-pawn becomes a target. Note 16...Nb4 fails to 17.Rd2! since 17...Nxa2 18.Ra1 wins. The text blocks action of the Bf4, but at the cost of permanently weakening d5) **15.Be3 Be6 16.b3 axb3 17.axb3 Rfd8** (White's plan is to advance the b-pawn to attack Black's Queenside pawns) **18.N1d2 f6** (The tempting 18...Rd3 is repulsed by 19.Rdc1 followed by 20.Bf1. Another important stratagem for White appears: the exchange of his less mobile KB for Black's Be6 by means of Bf1-c4. Then White's remaining Be3 will clearly outshine Black's hampered Bg7) **19.Bf1 Bf8 20.b4 Ra3?** (A serious mistake. Necessary was 20...cxb4 21.cxb4 allowing the use of d4 for Black's pieces) **21.bxc5** (Another defect of the omission of 20...cxb4 is that White now has use of the open b-file) **21...bxc5 22.Rdc1 Nc8 23.Bc4** (Well-timed; now 23...Kf7 fails to 24.Rb7+ winning the c5-pawn) **23...Bxc4 24.Nxc4 Ra4 25.Nfd2 Nd6 26.Nb6 Ra2 27.Ra1 Rxa1 28.Rxa1 f5 29.Nd5 fxe4?!** (Better was 29...Kf7) **30.Nf6+** (Now the additional weakness of e4 gives White a big positional advantage) **30...Kf7 31.Nfxe4 Nf5 32.Ra6 Nxe3 33.fxe3 Nb8 34.Rf6+ Ke7 35.Rb6 Nd7 36.Rc6 Ra8 37.Kf2 Ra2 38.Ke2 Kd8 39.Kd3** (White's King makes use of the weakened light squares to invade) **39...Be7 40.h4 Nb8 41.Re6 Nd7 42.Nc4 Rg2 43.Na5 Bf8 44.Nc6+ Kc7 45.Nxe5 Nxe5 46.Rxe5 Kd8 47.h5 Be7 48.hxg6 hxg6 49.Re6 g5 50.Re5 Kd7 51.Kc4 Rg1 52.Nxg5 Rxg3 53.Ne4 Rh3**

54.Nxc5+ Kd8 55.Ne6+ Kd7 56.Nd4 Bf6 57.Rf5 Ke7 58.Kd3 Rh1 59.c4 Ra1 60.Rb5 Ra3+ 61.Ke4 Kd7 62.Rb7+ Kc8 63.Rb3 Ra1 64.Kd5 Rd1 65.c5 Black Resigns.

Game 9
Ljubojevic-Kasparov
Niksic 1983

1.e4 c5 2.Nf3 e6 3.d3 Nc6 4.g3 d5 5.Nbd2 g6 6.Bg2 Bg7 7.0-0 Nge7 8.Re1 b6 9.h4 h6 10.c3 (10.Nf1!?. Dolmatov) **10...a5 11.a4 Ra7 12.Nb3!?** (Playable but probably not best. More dynamic was 12.exd5 and next Nb3 – see Game 6) **12...d4 13.cxd4** (Probably better was 13.e5) **13...cxd4 14.Bd2?** (A clumsy move which gives Black a big plus. 14.e5 was the right way. See Game 32 for the e5 push in a very similar position)

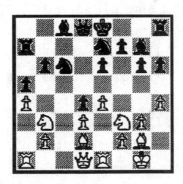

14...e5! (Now e5 is permanently blocked, leaving White with no play. Black will complete development and then advance the f-pawn [f5-f4] to obtain a powerful attacking game) **15.Nc1?!** (Better was 15.h5) **15...Be6 16.Re2 0-0 17.Be1** (White has allowed his pieces to be tied in knots. He has no counterplay and must stand by as Black's f-pawn stifles White's Kingside) **17...f5 18.Nd2 f4!** (The rest of the game is an instructive rout) **19.f3** (Hoping to block the attack with 20.g4. After 19.gxf4 exf4 the e5-square would fall into Black's hands) **19...fxg3 20.Bxg3 g5!** (Kasparov astutely sacrifices a pawn to open key lines and squares for the final attack) **21.hxg5 Ng6! 22.gxh6 Bxh6 23.Nf1 Rg7 24.Rf2 Be3!** (Crushing. Now after 25.Nxe3 dxe3 26.Rf1 Qg5 27.Ne2 Nf4 it's over) **25.b3 Nf4 White Resigns.**

Game 10
Benjamin-Eingorn
St. John 1988

1.e4 e6 2.d3 c5 3.Nf3 Nc6 4.g3 d5 5.Nbd2 g6 6.Bg2 Bg7 7.0-0 Nge7 8.Re1 h6 (We have seen this several times before; now 9.e5? is met by 9...g5!) **9.h4 b6 10.c3 a5** (On 10...Ba6?! 11.Qa4! looks good: 11...Bxd3 12.exd5 exd5? 13.Qxc6+, or 12...Qxd5 13.Ne5) **11.a4** (Dolmatov likes 11.Nf1 – see Game 8) **11...Ba6** (The usual 11...Ra7 is better) **12.exd5!** (Beginning play against Black's central and Queenside pawn structure) **12...exd5 13.Nb3** (Preparing d4) **13...0-0 14.d4 c4** (After 14...cxd4 15.Nbxd4 leaves Black with an isolated d-pawn) **15.Nbd2** (So White's QN has lost some time, but in return Black's pawns are compromised) **15...Bc8** (But Black also has to invest time to relocate the QB) **16.Nf1 Be6 17.Bf4 Qd7 18.b3!** (Pressuring the pawns. Now probably 18...Rad8 was best) **18...cxb3 19.Qxb3** (The b6-pawn is very weak, so Black foregoes the very passive 19...Nc8 in favor of some counterplay, but White holds the higher cards here) **19...f6 20.Qxb6** (Naturally!) **20...g5 21.hxg5 hxg5 22.Bc1 Rfc8 23.Qb5 Rab8 24.Qe2 Nd8** (Defending the Be6, while trying to pressure White's c-pawn and hoping to shift pieces to the center and Kingside) **25.Bxg5?!**

(see next diagram)

(Over-anxious. Good was the simple 25.Ne3 and if 25...Rxc3 then 26.Bd2 and 27.Bxa5) **25...fxg5 26.Nxg5 Rb6 27.Qd3** (On 27.Qh5 Black has 27...Rxc3 28.Rxe6 Rxe6 29.Bh3 Rh6! 30.Qxh6 Bxh6 31.Bxd7 Bxg5) **27...Qe8 28.Ne3 Qh5 29.f4 Bf7 30.Bf3 Qg6 31.Qxg6 Rxg6** (With three pawns for the piece White has achieved an approximately equal

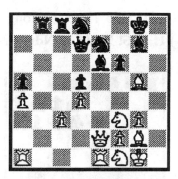

After 25.Bxg5?!

ending) **32.Ra3 Rd6 33.Nxf7 Kxf7 34.Rb3 Ne6 35.Kg2 Rcc6?!** (Better was 35...Rc7, preventing 36.Rb7) **36.Rb7** (Threatening to take the d-pawn) **36...Nc7 37.Bh5+ Kg8 38.Rb8+ Bf8?** (Another error. Better was 38...Kh7) **39.Ng4 Nf5** (39...Kg7 40.Re5!) **40.Re5 Ng7 41.Rg5 Ne6 42.Nf6+ Kh8 43.Rg6 Nxf4+** (Forced) **44.gxf4 Rxf6 45.Rxf8+!** (Forcing an easily won Rook and pawn ending) **45...Rxf8 46.Rxc6 Nxh5 47.Rh6+ Kg7 48.Rxh5 Rc8 49.Rxd5 Rxc3 50.Rxa5 Rc4 51.Kf3 Rxd4 52.Kg4 Black Resigns.**

Game 11
Pavlenko-Trubitsyn
Correspondence 1988/91

   1.e4 e6 2.d3 d5 3.Nd2 c5 4.g3 Nc6 5.Bg2 g6 6.Ngf3 Bg7 7.0-0 Nge7 8.Re1 b6 9.exd5! (In true hypermodern style, White gives up his central e-pawn in order to strike back at Black's center) **9...exd5** (9...Nxd5 10.d4! cxd4 11.Nb3 Bb7 12.Nfxd4 Nxd4 13.Nxd4 Rc8 14.Rxe6+!! fxe6 15.Nxe6 Qd7 16.Nxg7+, analysis by Oratovski) **10.d4! c4** (After 10...cxd4 11.Nb3 White recovers his pawn with pressure against Black's isolated d-pawn. Or 10...Nxd4 11.Nxd4 Bxd4 12.Nb3 Bg7 13.Bxd5 in White's favor; while 10...Bxd4 11.Nxd4 is clearly too dangerous, leaving the dark-squares completely under White's control. Finally, if 10...0-0 then 11.dxc5 bxc5 12.Nb3! Qb6 13.c3 is strong for White, Oratovski-Kirjakov, Vejen 1993) **11.Ne5! Nxd4 12.Ndxc4 Ne6**

13.Bg5!! (White plays with great energy. Now if 13...Nxg5 then 14.Nc6 wins, while 13...Bb7 is mashed by 14.Nxf7!! Kxf7 15.Qf3+) **13...f6 14.Nc6!** (The "positional" KIA has become as violent as a 19th century King's Gambit!) **14...Nxc6 15.Bxd5 Nb4 16.Bxe6** (16.Bxa8 is answered by 16...Qxd1 17.Raxd1 fxg5 18.Nd6+ Ke7) **16...Qxd1 17.Raxd1 Bxe6 18.Rxe6+ Kf7 19.Re4! Rhd8** (19...fxg5 20.Nd6+ and 21.Rxb4) **20.Ne5+ Kg8 21.Rxd8+ Rxd8 22.Rxb4 fxg5 23.Nc6?!** (An unfortunate inaccuracy after so many brilliant moves. Correct was 23.Nd3 with a clear advantage) **23...Rd2! 24.c3 Bf8 25.Rb5 Bc5 26.Nxa7 g4 27.Nc6 Bxf2+ 28.Kf1 Bc5 29.b4 Rf2+ 30.Ke1 Rb2 31.Ne5** (Better was 31.a4 and if 31...Bg1 then 32.Nd4 with an edge for White) **31...Bg1 32.Nxg4 h5 33.Nf6+ Kf7 34.Ne4 Rxa2 35.h3 Ke6 36.Ng5+** (Not 36.Rg5 Be3! 37.Rxg6+? Kf5) **36...Kf6 37.g4 hxg4 38.hxg4 Be3 39.Ne4+ Ke6 40.Ng5+ Kd6 41.Nf7+ Kc7 42.Rd5 Rc2** (Black has just enough activity to hold the draw) **43.Rd3 Bf4 44.g5 Rc1+ 45.Ke2 Rc2+ 46.Ke1 Draw.**

Game 12
Dvoretsky-Chubinsky
Philadelphia 1990

1.e4 c5 2.Nf3 e6 3.d3 Nc6 4.g3 g6 5.d4!? (The sharpest attempt. The basic idea is that the loss of time implicit in the double march of the d-pawn is justified by the weakening of d6 [neither the Black KB, soon to be placed on g7, nor the e6-pawn will be able to guard this square]; by way of comparison, after the standard early moves of the Sicilian Dragon Variation [1.e4 c5 2.Nf3 d6 3.d4 cxd4 4.Nxd4 Nf6 5.Nc3 g6 and 6...Bg7], the square d6 is firmly protected by the e7-pawn) **5...cxd4** (The most usual. Not so good is 5...Bg7?! 6 dxc5 Qa5+ 7.Bd2! Qxc5 8.Bc3, leaving Black's dark-squares in bad shape. However, Black can go in for Dvoretsky's dynamic pawn sac after 5...cxd4 6.Nxd4 Bg7! 7.Nb5 d5 8.exd5 exd5 9.Qxd5 Qe7+! 10.Be2 Bg4!. Only further testing can decide the issue) **6.Nxd4 a6** (Obviously, Nb5 must be stopped) **7.Bg2 Qc7** (7...Bg7 8.Nxc6 bxc6 [8...dxc6 9.Qxd8+ Kxd8 10.Nd2! and the weak dark-squared complex a5/b6/c5/d6 is too exposed.] 9.0-0 Ne7 [Trying to cover the weakness at d6 by 9...d5 fails to 10.exd5 cxd5 11.c4 and Black's position is cracking.] 10.Qd6! with a strong bind, Dvoretsky-Filipovic, Varna, 1980) **8.0-0 Bg7 9.Be3 Nge7 10.c4** (White sets up the famous Maroczy Bind pawn structure, figuring the considerable advantage in space gained thereby, coupled with Black's weak dark-squares and somewhat awkward piece layout, must give him a clear plus) **10...0-0 11.Nc3 d6**

(see next diagram)

(Trying to win a pawn by 11...Nxd4 12.Bxd4 Qxc4 13.Bxg7 Kxg7 14.Rc1 is terribly risky; Black could hardly complete his Queenside development while White's initiative would continue to grow unchecked) **12.Rc1 Nxd4** (It's hard to find a good plan for Black; after 12...b6 13.Nd5! exd5 14.cxd5 Black is lost) **13.Bxd4 e5?** (A strategical

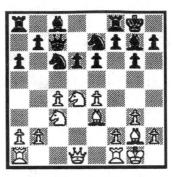

After 11...d6

error, obstructing his own Bg7 while leaving White's good QB to roam freely. Relatively better was 13...Bxd4 and only then ...e5) **14.Be3 Be6 15.Nd5 Bxd5 16.cxd5** (Now White has added the two Bishops and potential control of the c-file to his assets) **16...Qd7 17.Qb3 f5?!** (Allowing the following blockade of the Queenside is hopeless. He had to try 17...b5 and pray) **18.Qb6! Rac8 19.Bh3** (Exploiting the absence of Black's QB) **19...Rxc1 20.Rxc1 Rc8 21.b3 Rxc1+ 22.Bxc1 Nc8 23.Qe3 Ne7 24.Qc3 Kf7 25.a4** (White patiently increases his grip on the position) **25...Qd8 26.Qf3! Qd7 27.g4! Qc7 28.Ba3 f4 29.g5** (Now the h3-c8 diagonal is the basis for a decisive invasion) **29...h5 30.gxh6 e.p. Bxh6 31.Qg4 Ke8 32.Qe6 Qc2 33.Bxd6 Black Resigns.**

Game 13
Ljubojevic-Timman
Hilversum 1973

1.e4 e6 2.d3 c5 3.Nf3 Nc6 4.g3 g6 5.Bg2 Bg7 6.0-0 Nge7 7.c3 (Preparing to play d4) **7...0-0** (Preferable were both 7...d5, transposing into standard Sicilian System lines, or 7...e5 [for which see Game 17]. Both of these moves prevent an immediate d4) **8.d4! cxd4** (For 8...d6 see Game 15) **9.cxd4 d5** (After 9...Qb6?! 10.d5! Bxb2 11.dxc6 Bxa1 12.cxd7 White comes out on top) **10.e5** (White has achieved a favorable center pawn wedge which smothers the Bg7 and creates preconditions for a strong Kingside attack) **10...Nf5** (For 10...f6 see Game 14) **11.Nc3** (Note that the omission of an early Nbd2 has allowed the QN to assume this more aggressive post) **11...f6** (Trying to challenge White's center, but it stands "like a house") **12.Re1 fxe5 13.dxe5 Bd7 14.Bf4** (White's minor pieces are all centrally directed, creating a harmonious impression; on the other hand, Black's Bishops are cramped out of active play)

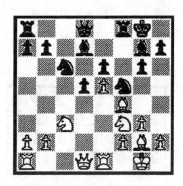

14...h6 15.h4 Be8 (Preparing 16...Qb6. If 15...Qb6? then 16.Nxd5!) **16.Qd2 Qb6 17.Rad1** (Now every White piece is beautifully centralized!) **17...Rd8 18.Na4!** (The QN eyes a fine post at c5 while "bumping" the Queen) **18...Qb5 19.b3 Kh7 20.Bf1** (Forcing Black into a poor ending) **20...Qb4 21.Qxb4 Nxb4 22.Nc5 Bf7 23.a3!** (Winning material) **23...b6** (23...Nc6 24.Nxb7 Rb8 25.Ba6) **24.axb4 bxc5 25.bxc5 Rb8 26.Rb1 a5 27.Bd2 Rfc8 28.Rec1 g5 29.Bd3 g4 30.Nd4 Bg6 31.Nxf5 Bxf5 32.Bxf5+ exf5 33.Bxa5 Bxe5 34.b4 Rb5 35.Rd1 d4 36.Kf1 Re8 37.Re1 Re7 38.Rbd1 Kg6 39.Rxd4 Bxd4 40.Rxe7 Kf6 41.Bd8 Black Resigns.**

Game 14
Ljubojevic-Tatai
Manila 1973

1.e4 e6 2.d3 c5 3.Nf3 Nc6 4.g3 g6 5.Bg2 Bg7 6.0-0 Nge7 7.c3 0-0?! (Better 7...d5 or 7...e5) **8.d4 cxd4 9.cxd4 d5 10.e5 f6** (Trying to defend his Kingside by gaining some space there, but only White will really benefit. This game shows 7...0-0 is a significant positional error, leaving Black with few prospects of decent counterplay) **11.Re1 fxe5 12.dxe5 Bd7 13.Nc3 Rc8**

(Clearly Black hopes to obtain play on the c-file by ...Na5-c4. But, as we shall see, this is over-optimistic) **14.Bf4 Nf5 15.Qd2 Na5 16.b3** (Simple but very effective; Black's hoped for play on the c-file is neutralized, leaving White with a big positional advantage in the center and Kingside) **16...b5?** (Striving for counterplay on the Queenside, Black overlooks some effective tactics) **17.Bg5! Qb6** (17...Ne7 18.Nxb5! Bxb5 19.Bxe7 Qxe7 20.Qxa5 wins) **18.g4! Nh6** (Or 18...h6 19.gxf5 hxg5 20.f6 Bh6 21.h4) **19.Bxh6 Bxh6 20.Qxh6 Rxf3** (After 20...Rxc3 21.Ng5 Qxf2+ 22.Kh1 Rf7 23.Rf1 wins) **21.Bxf3 Rxc3 22.Qf4 Nc6 23.Bxd5!** (Ending all resistance: 23...exd5 24.e6 Be8 25.e7 Nxe7 26.Rxe7 Rc8 27.Rae1 wins easily) **23...Nd4 24.Rad1 Black Resigns.**

Game 15
Fischer-Durao
Havana Olympiad 1966

1.e4 e6 2.d3 c5 3.Nf3 Nc6 4.g3 g6 5.Bg2 Bg7 6.0-0 Nge7 7.c3 (Blocking the scope of the Bg7 and preparing the possibility of d4) **7...0-0?!** (Preferable was 7...d5 or 7...e5 [see Game 17 for this], as now White gets a strong pawn center) **8.d4! d6 9.dxc5!** (White has formed a strong pawn center: why does he immediately disintegrate it? The answer is that this pawn trade will lead to a set of transformations of the pawn structures in the Queenside and center which are strategically favorable for White. Thus, even though the pawn center has existed for only one move, it has served a vital purpose in leading toward these transformations. We shall examine these as they occur at various later stages of the game) **9...dxc5 10.Qe2 b6** (Stopping 11.e5 by 10...e5 only creates a weak point on d5) **11.e5**

(The first pawn structure change, cramping Black in the center and clearing e4 for White's pieces) **11...a5?!** (Lured by the prospect of harassing White's Queen by ...Ba6, Black permanently weakens b6 and b5) **12.Re1 Ba6 13.Qe4 Ra7 14.Nbd2 Bd3** (Superficial. Preferable was 14...Rd7) **15.Qh4** (With White's Queen now pressing on the Kingside, Black goes in for a Queen trade; but the resulting ending is a slow death due to the superior placement of White's pawns) **15...Nd5 16.Qxd8**

Rxd8 17.a4! (A key stratagem, fixing the weaknesses at b6 and b5)
17...Rad7 (This doubling looks impressive, but nothing will come of it;
meanwhile White maneuvers to exploit Black's weak squares and weak
pawns) **18.Bf1!** (Another strategical device – the trade of White's ham
pered KB for Black's good Bishop will allow inroads on the light-
squares) **18...Bxf1 19.Kxf1 Nde7 20.Nc4** (Direct pressure begins)
20...Nc8 21.Bg5 N6e7 (21...Re8 22.Rad1 and White takes over the d-file,
an ironic turn of events) **22.Nfd2** (Heading for e4) **22...h6 23.Bxe7!**
(Excellent! White realizes that Knights are more important than Bishops
in this position, because of the fixed pawn structure) **23...Rxe7 24.Ra3!
Rc7 25.Rb3 Rc6 26.Ne4** (The magnificent steeds dominate the board)
26...Bf8 27.Ke2 Be7 28.f4 Kf8 29.g4! (Another pawn structure change.
The ideas are to target the h6-pawn and keep Black worried over a
possible break with f4-f5) **29...Ke8 30.Rf1 Rd5 31.Rf3! Rd8 32.Rh3
Bf8** (Forced, but now the unguarded f6 allows a clever combination)
33.Nxa5! Rc7 (33...bxa5? allows mate in four) **34.Nc4 Ra7 35.Nxb6
Nxb6 36.Rxb6 Rda8 37.Nf6+ Kd8 38.Rc6 Rc7 39.Rd3+ Kc8
40.Rxc7+ Kxc7 41.Rd7+ Kc6 42.Rxf7 Black Resigns.**

Game 16
Fischer-Panno
Buenos Aires 1970

   1.e4 c5 2.Nf3 e6 3.d3 Nc6 4.g3 g6 5.Bg2 Bg7 6.0-0 Nge7 7.Re1 (In
the last three games we saw 7.c3 as a preparation for d4. We believe that
7.c3 is the more accurate course – if White is steering for an early d4.
See note to Black's 10th for detailed analysis) **7...d6** (To stop 8.e5. For
7...0-0?! 8.e5! see Game 26) **8.c3 0-0 9.d4?!** (This is not convincing in
the given position. Hence White should consider 9.Na3!? with interesting play) **9...cxd4 10.cxd4 d5?!** (Allowing White to consolidate his
center. Correct was Huebner's 10...Qb6!; e.g. 11.d5 Bxb2 12.Bxb2 Qxb2
13.dxc6 [13.Nbd2 Na5 14.Qa4 Qb6 15.e5 Nxd5 16.exd6 Qd8 favors

Black.] 13...Qxa1 14.Qb3 Nxc6 15.Nc3 Nd4 16.Rxa1 Nxb3 17.axb3 Bd7 with an edge for Black, Ljubojevic-Huebner, Buenos Aires 1978) **11.e5 Bd7 12.Nc3 Rc8 13.Bf4 Na5** (This Knight maneuver leads nowhere, but Black is always inferior in such positions as we have seen in Games 13 and 14) **14.Rc1 b5 15.b3!** (Shutting out the Na5) **15...b4 16.Ne2 Bb5** (16...Rxc1 17.Nxc1 and Nd3) **17.Qd2 Nac6?** (Trying to get the errant Knight back into play, but he should have tried 17...Bxe2 to simplify) **18.g4!** (A fine constricting move leaving the Ne7 hemmed-in. Also, White wishes to shift the QN into the attack zone by Ng3. Therefore, Black had to play 18...Bxe2 now to have any chances of defense) **18...a5?! 19.Ng3 Qb6 20.h4** (A formidable armada of pieces and pawns are approaching the Black King)

20...Nb8 21.Bh6 (Invading on the dark-squares) **21...Nd7 22.Qg5 Rxc1 23.Rxc1 Bxh6 24.Qxh6 Rc8** (Black is trying desperately to pare off pieces and defend with only minor pieces and Queens left. But White's position is still too strong on the Kingside, though crisp tactical play is required to break through) **25.Rxc8+ Nxc8 26.h5 Qd8** (Hoping to play 27...Qf8) **27.Ng5** (Forcing 27...Nf8 and stopping ...Qf8) **27...Nf8 28.Be4!!** (A problem-like tactical motif cracks the Black defenses. Now 28...dxe4 loses after 29.N3xe4 Qe7 30.Nf6+ Kh8 31.Ngxh7) **28...Qe7 29.Nxh7!** (A piquant follow-up) **29...Nxh7 30.hxg6 fxg6** (Or 30...Nf8 31.g7) **31.Bxg6 Ng5** (31...Be8 32.Bxh7+ Qxh7 33.Qxe6+ Kf8 34.Qxc8

Qb1+ 35.Kg2 Qxa2 36.Nf5 wins) **32.Nh5! Nf3+ 33.Kg2 Nh4+ 34.Kg3 Nxg6 35.Nf6+! Kf7 36.Qh7+ Black Resigns.**

Game 17
Geller-Spassky
Alekhine Memorial 1971

1.e4 c5 2.Nf3 e6 3.d3 Nc6 4.g3 d6 5.Bg2 g6 6.0-0 (6 d4!? is similar to Game 12) **6...Bg7 7.c3 e5** (Preventing 8.d4, but the double move of the e6-pawn costs time) **8.a3** (To try for more space on the Queenside with b4. A sharper idea, trying to exploit Black's loss of time on move 7, is 8.Nh4!?; e.g., 8...Nge7 9.f4 exf4 10.gxf4 f5 [10...0-0 11.f5] 11.exf5 Nxf5 12.Re1+ Kf7 13.Nf3 and Black's exposed King gives White good chances) **8...Nf6** (After 8...a5 9.a4! White has good play against b5, b6 and c4 – e.g., Na3-b5 and Nfd2-c4, or Na3-c4) **9.b4 0-0 10.b5 Ne7** (Best. On 10...Na5 11.c4 leaves the Knight poorly placed) **11.a4 a6** (Fighting for some territory on the Queenside) **12.Na3 axb5 13.Nxb5 Nc6** (Better was 13...h6 to stop the next move) **14.Bg5!**

(A fine strategical move, designed to remove the Nf6 in order to gain more control over d5) **14...h6 15.Bxf6 Bxf6 16.Nd2!** (On the way toward d5 via c4 and e3) **16...Na7** (To exchange off the unpleasant visitor) **17.Na3** (Correctly avoiding exchanges to maintain pressure) **17...Nc6** (A tacit invitation to a repetition after 18.Nb5 Na7; but Geller declines)

18.Rb1 Bg7 19.N2c4 Ra6 20.Ne3 Ne7 21.Nac4 Bd7 22.a5 (Keeping the b7-pawn as a fixed target) **22...Bc6 23.Qb3 h5!** (To get his bad KB into active play) **24.Nd5!** (A precisely-timed occupation of d5. Now 23...Nxd5? 24.exd5 wins the b-pawn, while 23...Bxd5 24.exd5 leaves the b-pawn very weak – e.g., Qb5, Rb3 and Rfb1) **24...Bh6 25.f4 exf4 26.gxf4 Bxd5!** (Spassky shows characteristic resourcefulness; he sacs the b-pawn to obtain counterplay. The main idea is that now f5 is available for his Knight) **27.exd5 Nf5 28.Be4?!** (Both sides were in time pressure here. Correct was 28.Qxb7! and the onus is on Black to show any real compensation for the pawn) **28...Bxf4! 29.Bxf5** (29.Rxf4 Qg5+) **29...Qg5+ 30.Kh1 Qxf5 31.Qxb7 Re8?** (A clever but unsound Rook sac. He should sac the other Rook with 31...Ra7!! to divert the Queen from protecting d5, e.g., 32.Qxa7 Qxd5+ 33.Kg1 Qg5+ 34.Kh1 Qd5+ with perpetual check) **32.Rf2!** (An excellent defensive move – in time pressure! Now 32...Ra7 fails after 33.Qxa7 Qxd5+ 34.Kg1 Qg5+ [34...Qxd3 Rbf1] 35.Kf1; or, 33...Qxd3 34.Rbf1 Qxd5+ 35.Kg1 g5 36.Qa6) **32...g5 33.Rg1?!** (33.Qxa6! Qxd5+ 34.Kg1 Qxd3 35.Qb5) **33...Rea8?** (Time pressure again. Instead 33...h4! since 34.Qxa6? loses to 34...Qxd5+ 35.Rfg2 h3) **34.Nxd6!** (Now White is winning again) **34...Rxd6 35.Qxa8+ Kh7 36.c4 Rf6** (36...Qxd3 37.Rxf4! gxf4 38.Qg8+ leads to mate) **37.Qb7 Qh3** (37...Qxd3 38.Qb1) **38.Qb2!** (Not 38.a6? Bxh2! 39.Rxh2 Qf3+ and it's a perpetual check) **38...Be5 39.Qe2** and Black lost on time.

Game 18
Oratovski-Maiwald
Vejen 1993

1.e4 e6 2.d3 d5 3.Nd2 c5 4.g3 Nc6 5.Bg2 g6 6.Ngf3 Bg7 7.0-0 Nge7 8.Re1 0-0 9.h4 h6 10.e5 f5?! 11.exf6 e.p. Rxf6 12.Nh2 (Not bad, but we think 12.Nf1! is best. See Game 5) **12...Rf7 13.Ng4 Qd6 14.Nb3 Kh7 15.c4** (Pressuring Black's center) **15...Bd7?!** (Oratovski gives

15...b6 16.Be3 Bb7 17.Qc1 – unclear) **16.Be3 b6** (After 16...d4 the e4 square becomes a fine outpost for White's pieces; but this may have been Black's best choice) **17.d4!**

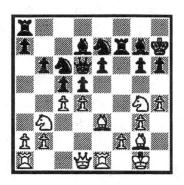

(White forces the dissolution of Black's pawn center with this dynamic move) **17...dxc4 18.dxc5 Qxd1 19.Raxd1 Nd5** (On 19...cxb3 20.Rxd7 bxa2? 21.Bxc6 wins) **20.Nd4 Ncb4!?** (After 20...Nxd4 21.Bxd4 Bxd4 22.Rxd4 bxc5 23.Rxc4 Black's position is decimated. On 20...h5 21.Nxc6! Bxc6 22.Bd4!! Bxd4 23.Rxd4 bxc5 24.Rdd1 Ba4 [24...hxg4 25.Rxe6 wins back the piece with a positionally won game due mainly to Black's shattered pawn structure.] 25.Rxd5! exd5 26.Bxd5 Re8 27.Rxe8 Bxe8 28.Bxf7 Bxf7 29.Nf6+ Kg7 30.Ne4 and the Knight mops up on Black's pawns. Finally, if 20...Nxe3 then 21.Rxe3 Bxd4 22.Rxd4! Nxd4 23.Bxa8 bxc5 24.Ne5 Re7 25.Be4 Nf5 26.Ra3 and despite Black's extra pawn his game is lost because his pawns are catastrophically weak and all of White's pieces are on far better posts. Another example of how the "quiet, positional" KIA can suddenly switch into a series of beautiful tactical blows – based on variations by Oratovski) **21.c6!** (After seeing his "heavier" colleagues pound the Black position, the c-pawn cannot resist doing its share. Now 21...Nxc6 22.Nxc6 Bxc6 23.Bd4! wins; the extra pawn is no compensation–White's pieces zero in on the many weak pawns and weak squares in Black's position) **21...Bc8 22.Be4!** (Threatening 23.h5) **22...Rf5!** (Black fights back resourcefully. Now on 23.Nxf5

Oratovski gives 23...gxf5 24.Bxd5 Nxd5 with counterplay) **23.Bc1!** (But this calm retreat keeps up the pressure) **23...Rh5?** (Oratovski gives 23...Nxa2 24.Bxf5 gxf5 25.Ne5 with a big advantage for White; White's horses rule the center) **24.a3 e5 25.Nb5 Bxg4 26.f3!** (This forceful finesse ends Black's stubborn resistance as 26...Bxf3 27.Bxf3 leaves most of Black's pieces hanging) **26...Be6 27.axb4 a6 28.Bxd5 Bxd5 29.Rxd5 axb5 30.c7** (Threat: 31.Rd8) **30...Rc8 31.g4!** (Forcing the Rook to give up control of e5) **31...Rxh4 32.Rd7** (Now the threat of 33.Rxe5 and 34.Ree7 is too much to handle – if 32...g5 then 33.Rxe5 Kg6 34.Re6+ Bf6 35.Rxb6 and Rb8) **Black Resigns.**

Game 19
Sax-Nogueiras
Rotterdam (World Cup) 1989

1.e4 e6 2.d3 d5 3.Nd2 c5 4.Ngf3 Nc6 5.g3 Nge7 6.Bg2 g6 7.0-0 Bg7 8.Re1 b6 9.c3 a5 10.exd5 exd5 11.d4 cxd4 12.Nxd4 Nxd4 13.cxd4 0-0

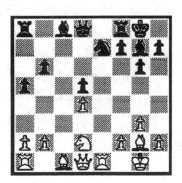

14.Nc4 Nf5 15.Ne5 Be6 16.h4 Rc8 17.Bf4 Re8 18.Bf1 Nd6 19.Rc1 Nc4 20.b3 Nxe5 21.Rxc8 Draw.

Game 20
Xie-Brunner
Germany 1992

1.e4 c5 2.Nf3 e6 3.d3 Nc6 4.g3 g6 5.Bg2 Bg7 6.0-0 Nge7 7.c3 0-0
8.Be3!? (8.Re1; 8.d4!?) 8...d6 9.Na3 b6 10.d4 cxd4 11.Nxd4 Bb7
12.Qa4 d5

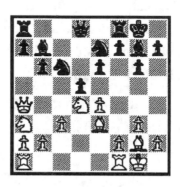

13.exd5 Nxd4 14.Bxd4 Bxd4 15.Qxd4 Bxd5 16.Rfd1 Bxg2 17.Kxg2
Qc7 18.Qd7 (+=) 18...Qxd7 19.Rxd7 Nd5 20.Rd1 Rfd8 21.Rxd8+
Rxd8 22.Kf3 (22.c4?? Ne3+) 22...Rc8 23.Ke2 Kf8 24.Rd4 Ke7 25.Ra4
a5 26.Rc4 Rxc4 27.Nxc4 a4 28.Kd3 f6 29.Ne3 b5 30.Nc2 Kd6 31.c4!
Nb6 32.cxb5 e5 33.f4 exf4 34.gxf4 Kc5 35.Nd4 Nc4 36.b3 axb3
37.axb3 Nd6 38.Ne6+ Kxb5 39.Nf8 Kb4 40.Nxh7 Ne8 41.Kd4 Kxb3
42.Kd5 g5 43.Nxg5! fxg5 44.fxg5 Ng7 45.h4 Nh5 46.Ke6 Kc4 47.g6
Kd4 48.Kf7 **Black Resigns.**

Game 21
Yurtaev-Dolmatov
U.S.S.R. 1984

1.e4 e6 2.d3 c5 3.Nf3 Nc6 4.g3 g6 5.Bg2 Bg7 6.0-0 Nge7 7.c3 d5
8.Nbd2 b6 9.Re1 h6 10.e5?! (10.h4!) 10...Qd7 (10...g5!) 11.d4 cxd4
12.cxd4 Ba6 13.a3! g5 (13...0-0!?) 14.Nf1 Nf5 15.g4! Nfe7 16.Ng3

0-0-0 17.b4 f5 18.gxf5 Nxf5 (18...exf5 19.Nh5 Rhg8 20.Nf6!) **19.Nxf5 exf5**

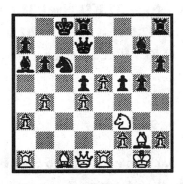

20.e6?! (20.a4! Nxb4 21.Ba3) **20...Qd6?** (20...Qc7! =) **21.a4! g4** (21...Nxb4 22.Ba3 +-) **22.Nh4 Nxd4 23.b5! Nf3+ 24.Nxf3 Bxa1 25.Nd4! Bb7 26.Nxf5 Qc7 27.e7 Black Resigns.**

Game 22
Ljubojevic-Petrosian
Milano 1975

1.e4 e6 2.d3 d5 3.Nd2 c5 4.Ngf3 Nc6 5.g3 Nge7 6.Bg2 g6 7.0-0 Bg7 8.Re1 b6 9.a3 h6 10.Rb1 a5 11.h4 Ba6?! (11...a4) 12.exd5 Nxd5 (12...exd5 13.d4!) 13.Nc4 0-0 14.Nce5 Rc8 15.Nxc6 Rxc6 16.c4! Ne7 17.Bf4 b5 18.Qc1 h5 19.Ne5 Rc8 20.b4! cxb4 21.axb4 a4 22.Qe3 Nf5 23.Qa7 Ra8 24.Qc5! Rc8

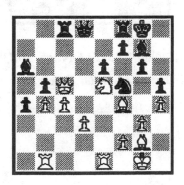

25.Nc6 Qd7 26.cxb5 Bb7 27.Be5 Bxe5 28.Nxe5 Qd8 29.Nc6 Qxd3 30.Be4 Qd6 31.Qxd6 Nxd6 32.Ne7+ Kg7 33.Nxc8 Nxe4 34.Nb6 Nd2 35.Nxa4 Rb8 36.Rbc1 Nf3+ 37.Kf1 Nxe1 38.Kxe1 Ra8 39.Nc5 Bd5 40.b6 Rb8 41.Nd7 Ra8 42.Rc7 Ra1+ 43.Kd2 Ra2+ 44.Ke3 e5 45.b7 Ra3+ 46.Kd2 Ra2+ 47.Kc3 Black Resigns.

Game 23
Z.Nikolic-Hulak
Yugoslavia 1991

1.e4 c5 2.Nf3 e6 3.d3 Nc6 4.Nbd2 g6 5.g3 Bg7 6.Bg2 Nge7 7.h4 (Sharp, but it weakens the g4-square. See note to White's 10th) **7...h6 8.0-0 d5 9.Re1 b6 10.c3** (10.exd5?! exd5 11.d4? cxd4 12.Nb3 Bg4! -+) **10...Qc7 11.Nf1 Bb7 12.Qe2 d4!?** (12...0-0 13.e5 +=; 12...0-0-0 13.e5 +=) **13.c4 e5 14.N1h2 f5 15.Nd2 h5 16.exf5! gxf5 17.a3 a5 18.Ndf3 Qd6 19.Ng5 Qg6 20.f4! 0-0-0 21.fxe5 Nxe5 22.Bf4 N7c6 23.b4! axb4 24.axb4 cxb4 25.Bd5 Rhe8 26.Qc2 Re7**

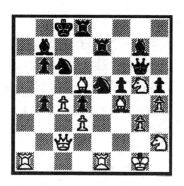

27.Qa4 Rde8 28.Red1 Nd7 29.Nhf3 Nde5 30.Qb5 Nd7 31.Rd2 Be5 32.Nxe5 Rxe5 33.Nf7 R5e6 34.Bxe6 Rxe6 35.Ng5 Re8 36.Rda2 Nc5 37.Qxb6 Black Resigns.

Game 24
Lau-Andruet
Wijk aan Zee B 1989

1.e4 c5 2.Nf3 e6 3.d3 Nc6 4.g3 g6 5.Bg2 Bg7 6.0-0 Nge7 7.c3 e5 8.a3 d6 (8...a5 9.a4! +=) 9.b4 0-0 10.Nbd2 h6 11.Bb2 Be6 12.Qe2 a6 13.Ne1 b5 14.Nc2 a5 15.bcx5 dxc5 16.a4! b4 17.c4 Nc8 18.Ne3 Qd6 19.f4 Rd8 20.f5 Bd7 (20...Qxd3 21.Qf3! Qxd2 22.Rf2 +-) 21.Nb3 Ra7 22.Nd5 Nd4 23.Bxd4 cxd4 24.Bh3 Be8 25.Rf2 Kh7 26.Qf1 Qb8 27.fxg6+ fxg6 28.Nc5! Rd6 29.Ne6 Ne7 30.Nxg7 Kxg7

31.Rf8 Nxd5 32.exd5 Qd8 33.Be6 Qe7 34.Rg8+ Kh7 35.Qf8 Qxf8 36.Rxf8 Re7 37.Raf1 Rdxe6 38.dxe6 Rxe6 39.R1f6 Rxf6 40.Rxf6 Bxa4 41.c5 Kg7 42.Ra6 b3 43.Rb6 Kf7 44.Kf2 Ke7 45.Kf3 b2 46.Ke4 Kd7 47.Rxb2 Kc6 48.Ra2 **Black Resigns.**

Game 25
Georgiev-B.Sanz
Palma Open 1989

1.e4 e6 2.d3 c5 3.Nf3 Nc6 4.Nbd2 g6?! 5.c3 Bg7? 6.Nb3!? (A relatively new idea: by attacking the c-pawn, White prepares to play an early d4 while eschewing the usual continuation, 6.g3. Hence 4...g6 [before White has committed himself to g3] is probably inaccurate. Therefore, preferable would have been 4...d5 or 5...d5) **6...b6 7.d4 cxd4**

8.cxd4 d5 9.e5 f6 10.Bb5 Bd7 11.Qe2 fxe5 12.Bxc6 Bxc6 13.Nxe5 Rc8 14.0-0 Nf6 15.Bd2 0-0 16.Rac1 Bb7

17.Nc6 Qd7 18.Nxa7 Rc4 19.a4 Ba6 20.a5 Rxc1 21.Qxa6 Rxf1+ 22.Kxf1 bxa5 23.Nc5 Qf7 24.Nb5 Nd7 25.Nd3 e5 26.Qxa5 Qf5 27.Qa3 exd4 28.Nd6 Qg4 29.Qb3 Qe6 30.Nb5 Rb8 31.Qa4 Qg4 32.Nc7 Qf5 33.Nb4 Rf8 34.f3 Qb1+ 35.Be1 Qxb2 36.Qxd7 d3 37.Qxd5+ Kh8 38.Qxd3 Bd4 39.Nc2 Bb6 40.Bc3+ Black Resigns.

Game 26
Petrosian-Pachman
Bled 1961

    1.e4 e6 2.d3 c5 3.Nf3 Nc6 4.g3 g6 5.Bg2 Bg7 6.0-0 Nge7 7.Re1 0-0?! (7...d5, 7...d6, or 7...e5 are correct) **8.e5!** (Now White has a definite plus) **8...d6 9.exd6 Qxd6 10.Nbd2 Qc7 11.Nb3! Nd4** (11...b6 12.Bf4) **12.Bf4 Qb6** (12...Nxf3+ 13.Bxf3 e5 14.Be3 c4 15.dxc4 Qxc4 16.Bc5 Re8 17.Bxe7 Rxe7 18.Qd8+ Bf8 19.Rxe5 winning) **13.Ne5 Nxb3 14.Nc4! Qb5 15.axb3 a5 16.Bd6! Bf6 17.Qf3! Kg7 18.Re4** (18.Qxf6+!! Kxf6 19.Be5+ Kg5 20.Bg7 e5 21.Rxe5+ Bf5 22.f4+ Kg4 23.Ne3+ Kh5 24.Bf3#) **18...Rd8**

19.Qxf6+!! Kxf6 20.Be5+ Kg5 21.Bg7!! Black Resigns (21...Nf5 22.f4+ Kg4 23.Ne5+ Kh5 24.Bf3#; or 21...e5 22.h4+ Kh5 23.Bf3+ Bg4 24.Bxg4#).

Game 27
Ljubojevic-Hort
Manila Interzonal 1976

    1.e4 e6 2.d3 c5 3.Nf3 Nc6 4.g3 g6 5.Bg2 Bg7 6.0-0 Nge7 7.Re1 d6 8.c3 e5 (8...0-0 9.d4?! cxd4 10.cxd4 Qb6!; 9.Na3!?) **9.a3 0-0** (9...a5 10.a4!) **10.b4 b6 11.Nbd2 a6 12.Rb1 Qc7 13.Nc4 b5 14.Ne3 Rb8 15.bxc5 dxc5 16.Nd5! Qd6 17.d4! Bg4 18.dxc5 Qxc5 19.Be3! Qd6 20.Nb4 Qxd1 21.Rexd1 Rfc8** (21...Nxb4 22.axb4!) **22.Nxa6 Ra8 23.Nc5 Rxa3 24.Rd3 Nd8 25.h3 Be6**

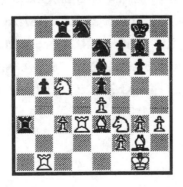

**26.Rxd8+! Rxd8 27.Nxe6 fxe6 28.Bc5 Rxc3 29.Bxe7 Rd7 30.Bb4
Rcd3 31.Be1 Rb7 32.Ng5 Rd6 33.Bf1 h6 34.Nf3 Rdb6 35.Ba5 Rc6
36.Bd2 Rc2 37.Rxb5 Rf7 38.Bd3 Rc8 39.Ne1 Rd7 40.Kf1 Kh7 41.Ke2
Rc6 42.h4 Ra7 43.Ba5 Rc1 44.Nf3 Ra1 45.Bc3 R1a2+ 46.Ke3 Rd7
47.Rb3 Black Resigns.**

Game 28
**Sax-Jansa
Madonna di Campiglio 1974**

**1.e4 c5 2.Nf3 e6 3.d3 Nc6 4.g3 g6 5.Bg2 Bg7 6.0-0 Nge7 7.c3 e5
8.Be3?! d6 9.a4 0-0 10.Nfd2 b6 11.Nc4 Be6 12.f4 exf4 13.Bxf4 d5
14.exd5 Nxd5 15.Bd6 Re8 16.Qf3 Rc8 17.Nbd2**

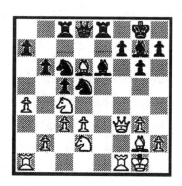

**17...Ne3! 18.Qxe3 Bxc4 19.Ne4 Bb3 20.Qf4 f5 21.Ra3 fxe4 22.Rxb3
g5! 23.Qf7+ Kh8 24.Bxc5 bxc5 25.Rb7 Re7 26.Rxe7 Nxe7 27.Bxe4
Qd6 28.Qh5 h6 29.Rf7 Rb8 30.Rf2 Qe6 31.Re2 Rf8 32.Bf3 Qf6
33.Kg2 Ng6 34.d4 cxd4 35.cxd4 Ne7 36.Qg4 Nf5 37.d5 Nd4 38.Rf2
Nxf3 39.Rxf3 Qxb2+ 40.Kh3 Rxf3 41.Qxf3 Qf6 42.Qe4 White
Resigns.**

Game 29
Yurtaev-Gulko
Moscow Olympiad 1994

1.e4 e6 2.d3 c5 3.Nf3 Nc6 4.g3 d5 5.Nbd2 Nge7 6.Bg2 g6 7.0-0 Bg7 8.Re1 b6 9.c3 Bb7 10.e5!? g5 11.Nxg5 Nxe5 12.Ndf3 N5g6 13.d4 h6 14.Nh3 Qd7 15.a4 Nc6 16.Nf4 Nxf4 17.Bxf4 Ba6 18.a5 Qb7 19.axb6 axb6 20.dxc5 bxc5

21.Qxd5 0-0 22.Qxc5 Qb5 23.Qe3 Qxb2 24.Rab1 Qc2 25.Bxh6 Bxh6 26.Qxh6 Rab8 27.Rbc1 Qf5 28.Nh4 Black Resigns.

Game 30
Komliakov-Seirawan
Moscow Olympiad 1994

1.e4 e6 2.d3 d5 3.Nd2 c5 4.Ngf3 Nc6 5.g3 Nge7 6.Bg2 g6 7.0-0 Bg7 8.Re1 b6 9.c3 a5 10.exd5 exd5 11.d4 a4 12.Ne5 Nxe5 13.dxe5 Be6 14.h4 h6 15.Nf3 0-0 16.Nh2 Qd7 17.Bf3 Kh7 18.Ng4 Ng8 19.Kg2 Rad8

(see next diagram)

20.Bg5 hxg5 21.hxg5 Bxg4 22.Bxg4 Qe7 23.Rh1+ Bh6 24.f4 d4 25.Rxh6+ Nxh6 26.Qh1 Rh8 27.gxh6 dxc3 28.bxc3 Rd2+ 29.Kf1

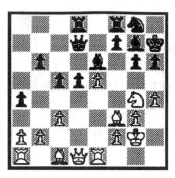

After 19...Rad8

Rhd8 30.Re1 Rxa2 31.Qe4 Rdd2 32.e6 f5 33.Bxf5 Rf2+ 34.Kg1 Rg2+ White Resigns.

Game 31
Shahwan-Ljubojevic
Moscow Olympiad 1994

1.e4 c5 2.Nf3 e6 3.d3 Nc6 4.g3 d5 5.Nbd2 g6 6.Bg2 Bg7 7.0-0 Nge7 8.Re1 h6 9.c3? (9.h4!) 9...dxe4 10.dxe4 g5! 11.Qe2 Qc7 12.h3 Ng6 13.Nf1 b6 14.Ne3 Bb7 15.Nc4 0-0 16.Ne3 Rad8 17.Ng4 Qd7 18.e5 Qd3 19.Qxd3 Rxd3 20.Nf6+ Kh8 21.h4 gxh4 22.gxh4 Na5 23.Be3

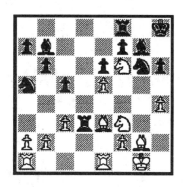

23...Bxf3 24.Bxf3 Nxe5 25.Be4 Bxf6 26.Bxh6 Rg8+ 27.Kf1 Rh3 28.Bg5 Bxg5 29.hxg5 Rh4 30.Bg2 Rxg5 31.Re3 Nac4 White Resigns.

Game 32
Damljanovic-Vehi Bach
San Sebastian Open 1994

1.Nf3 c5 2.e4 e6 3.d3 Nc6 4.g3 d5 5.Nbd2 g6 6.Bg2 Bg7 7.0-0 Nge7 8.Re1 b6 9.c3 a5 10.a4 Ra7 11.Nb3 d4 12.cxd4 cxd4 13.e5!? 0-0 14.Bd2 Ba6 15.Rc1 Rd7 16.Bg5 h6 17.Bxe7 Nxe7 18.Qe2 Bb7 19.Nfd2 Bxg2 20.Kxg2 Rd5 21.Nc4 g5 22.Nbd2 Ng6 23.Qh5 Nxe5 24.Nxe5 Bxe5 25.Qxh6 Bg7 26.Qh5 b5 27.axb5 Rxb5 28.b3 Qd5+ 29.Kg1 Rd8 30.Rc7 Qf5 31.g4 Qf4 32.Ra7 Rf8 33.Ne4 Re5 34.Kg2 Rc8 35.Re2 Rd5 36.Ra2 Re5

37.Rxf7 Qxf7 38.Qxf7+ Kxf7 39.Nd6+ Kg6 40.Nxc8 Rb5 41.Nd6 Rxb3 42.Rxa5 Rxd3 43.Ne4 Bf6 44.Ra6 Kf7 45.Ra7+ Kg6 46.Nc5 Rd1 47.Nxe6 Be5 48.Ra5 Kf6 49.Nc5 Bf4 50.Ne4+ Kg6 51.Rd5 d3 52.Nc3 Rd2 53.h3 Kf6 54.Ne4+ Ke6 55.Rxd3 Black Resigns.

Game 33
Wians-Schneider
Cappelle la Grande 1994

1.d3 c5 2.Nf3 Nc6 3.g3 g6 4.Bg2 Bg7 5.0-0 e6 6.e4 Nge7 7.c3 d5 8.Qe2 0-0 9.h4 h6 10.Nbd2?! (10.e5! +=) 10...e5! 11.a3 Bg4 12.b4 d4 13.Bb2 cxb4 14.cxb4 Nc8 15.Nb3 Nd6 16.Rfc1 a5 17.Nxa5 Nxa5

18.bxa5 Rxa5 19.Qe1 Rb5 20.Rc2 Qb6 21.Qc1 Rc8 22.Rxc8+ Bxc8 23.Rb1 Be6 24.Nd2

24...Ba2 25.Nc4 Nxc4 26.dxc4 Ra5 27.Ra1 Bxc4 28.Qxc4 Qxb2 29.Ra2 Qb1+ 30.Kh2 Bf8 31.h5 Rc5 32.Qe2 d3 33.Qb2 Qxb2 34.Rxb2 Rc2 35.Rxb7 Bc5 36.hxg6 fxg6 37.Rb3 d2 38.Rd3 Bxf2 39.Bf3 Bc5 40.Bd1 Rb2 41.Kg2 Kg7 42.Kf3 Ra2 43.Ke2 Kf6 44.a4 Bb4 45.Rb3 Ba5 46.Rb5 Bc3 47.Rb3 Bd4 48.Rd3 h5 49.Rxd2 Ra1 50.Bb3 Kg5 51.Ra2 Rb1 52.Be6 Rb6 53.Bc8 Rc6 54.Bd7 Rc3 55.a5 Rxg3 56.Ra4 h4 White Resigns.

Game 34
Bjornsson-Einarsson
Reykjavik Open 1994

   1.e4 e6 2.d3 d5 3.Nd2 c5 4.Ngf3 Nc6 5.g3 g6 6.Bg2 Bg7 7.0-0 Nge7 8.Re1 b6 9.e5?! Qc7 10.Qe2 g5! 11.Nxg5 Qxe5 12.Qxe5 Nxe5

(see next diagram)

13.Nc4 dxc4! 14.Bxa8 cxd3 15.cxd3 Nxd3 16.Re2 Ba6 17.Rc2 c4 18.Be4 Nc5 19.Be3 Na4 20.Rd1 h6 21.Rcd2 Nd5 22.Rxd5 exd5 23.Bxd5 0-0 24.Nxf7 Nxb2 25.Ne5+ Kh7 26.Be4+ Kg8 27.Bd5+ Kh7 28.Be4+ Draw.

After 12...Nxe5

Game 35
Ambroz-Barsov
Bern 1994

1.e4 e6 2.d3 d5 3.Nd2 c5 4.Ngf3 Nc6 5.g3 g6 6.Bg2 Bg7 7.0-0 Nge7
8.Re1 h6 9.c3 a5 10.a4 b6 11.exd5 exd5 12.d4 cxd4 13.Nxd4 Nxd4
14.cxd4 0-0 15.Nf3 Bf5 16.Ne5 Rc8 17.Qb3 g5 18.Bd2 Nc6 19.Bc3

19...Nxe5 20.dxe5 d4 21.Rad1 Qc7 22.Rxd4 Bxe5 23.Rd5 Rfe8
24.Rdxe5 Rxe5 25.Bxe5 Re8 Draw.

Game 36
Georgadze-Conquest
Calcutta Open 1994

1.Nf3 c5 2.g3 g6 3.Bg2 Bg7 4.0-0 Nc6 5.d3 d5 6.Nbd2 e6 7.e4 Nge7 8.Re1 h6 9.c3 b6 10.h4 Bb7 11.Qe2 Qd7 12.Nf1 dxe4 13.dxe4 0-0-0 14.Ne3 Qd3?! 15.Qxd3 Rxd3 16.Bf1 (+=) 16...Rd7 17.Nc4 b5 18.Ne3 a6 19.a4 c4 20.axb5 axb5 21.Nc2 f5 22.exf5 exf5 23.Be3 Nd5 24.Bd4 Nc7 25.Bxg7 Rxg7 26.Nfd4 f4 27.Nxc6 Bxc6 28.Nd4 Bd7 29.Ra7 g5 30.h5 g4 31.gxf4 Rf8 32.f5 g3 33.f4 Kb8 34.Rea1 g2 35.Be2 Rf6 36.Bf3 Rb6

37.Ne6 Black Resigns.

Game 37
Ljubojevic-Vaganian
Niksic 1978

1.e4 e6 2.d3 d5 3.Nd2 c5 4.Ngf3 Nc6 5.g3 g6 6.Bg2 Bg7 7.0-0 Nge7 8.Re1 b6 9.a3 Bb7 10.Rb1 Qc7 (10...a5!?) 11.b4 cxb4 12.axb4 a6 13.b5 axb5 14.Rxb5 Ra5 15.Rb3 dxe4 16.Nxe4 0-0 17.Bb2 e5 18.Qb1

(see next diagram)

18...Nc8 19.c4 Rd8 20.Nc3 N6a7! 21.Ba3 Bc6 22.Bb4 Ra6 23.Nd2 Bxg2 24.Kxg2 Nc6 25.Nd5 Qb7 26.Ne4 f5 27.Nec3 Nd4 28.Ra3 Draw.

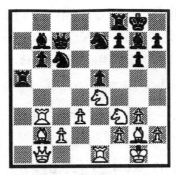

After 18.Qb1

Game 38
Kaidanov-A.Zapata
New York 1993

1.e4 c5 2.Nf3 e6 3.d3 d5 4.Nbd2 Nc6 5.g3 g6 6.Bg2 Bg7 7.0-0 Nge7
8.Re1 b6 9.c3 a5 10.a4 Ba6 11.exd5 Nxd5 (11...exd5 12.Nb3 and d4)
12.Nc4 (+=) 12...0-0 13.h4 Qc7 (13...h6!?) 14.h5 Rad8 15.Qe2 Rfe8
16.hxg6 hxg6 17.Ng5 e5 (17...f6? 18.Nxe6 Qd7 19.Bh3 followed by
20.Qf1 wins) 18.Qe4 Bb7 19.Qh4 Nf6 20.Ne4 Nh7! (20...Nxe4 21.dxe4
followed by Bg5 and Ne3-d5 is strong) 21.g4! (21.Re3 f5!) 21...Rxd3
22.Bf1 Rd7

(22...Rdd8 23.Re3 Qe7 24.g5 Bc8 25.Nxb6 Be6 26.Re1!) **23.Re3 Nd8?**
(23...g5! D.Gurevich: 24.Nxg5 [24.Qh5?! Nd8] 24...Nxg5 25.Qxg5 e4!?
[25...Rd1? 26.Rd3 Rd8?! 27.Rxd1 Rxd1 28.Ne3 Re1 29.Nf5 f6 30.Qg6

and Bh6 wins for White.] with counterplay) **24.Rh3 Bxe4 25.Qxh7 Kf8 26.Bh6 f6 27.Re1** (Not 27.Qh8+?? Kf7 28.Qxg7+ Ke6 and Black wins) **27...Qb7 28.g5! fxg5 29.Qh8+ Black Resigns.**

Game 39
Psakhis-Erdelyi
Lenk 1991

1.e4 c5 2.Nf3 e6 3.d3 Nc6 4.g3 g6 5.Bg2 Bg7 6.0-0 Nge7 7.Re1 d6 8.c3 e5 9.a3 a5 10.a4 h6 11.Na3 g5?! (11...0-0 12.Nd2! Be6 13.Ndc4 +=) **12.Nb5 Ng6** (12...0-0!? 13.Nd2! Be6 14.Nc4 Nc8 =+) **13.Nd2! Ra6** (13...Na7 14.Na3! 0-0 15.Ndc4 with advantage to White) **14.Nc4 Nce7 15.b4! axb4 16.cxb4 cxb4 17.Bd2 Be6 18.Bxb4 Nc8** (18...Bxc4 19.dxc4 with White on top) **19.Ne3 0-0 20.Nf5 Nge7 21.Nxg7! Kxg7 22.d4 Qb6 23.Bf1! f6 24.Qd2 Nc6 25.a5 Qd8 26.Bc3 Bg4 27.Rec1!** (27.d5 N6a7 28.Na3 f5! favors White, but the text is still stronger) **27...Qe7 28.Bb2 exd4 29.Nxd4 Ne5 30.Ra3 Ra8 31.f4** (+-) **31...Nf7 32.f5 Ne5 33.Ne6+ Kg8 34.Qd5 Rf7 35.Rc7 Qe8 36.Bxe5 dxe5**

37.Bb5 Ne7 38.Bxe8 Black Resigns.

Game 40
Csom-Afek
Budapest 1993

1.Nf3 c5 2.g3 Nc6 3.Bg2 g6 4.c3 e5 5.d3 Bg7 6.a3 Nge7 7.h4!? h6
8.b4 d6 (8...cxb4 9.axb4 Nxb4 [9...e4 10.dxe4 Nxb4 11.Nd4! with the
idea of Nb5.] 10.cxb4 e4 11.Ra2 exf3 12.Bxf3 +=) **9.e4 0-0 10.Be3**
cxb4?! (10...b6 =) **11.axb4 f5?** (11...d5 12.b5 d4 13.Bc1 +=) **12.Qd2 f4**
(12...Kh7 13.b5 Na5 [13...Nb8 14.Qa2 with 15.Ng5+!] 14.Ng5+! hxg5
15.hxg5+ Kg8 16.Qa2+ and 17.Qxa5) **13.gxf4 exf4 14.Bxf4 Kh7 15.Be3**
(15.b5 Ne5!) **15...Nxb4**

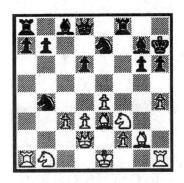

16.Ng5+!! hxg5 (16...Kg8 17.d4 Nbc6 18.Qa2+) **17.hxg5+ Kg8 18.cxb4**
Bxa1 19.Qa2+ Rf7 20.Qxa1 Rh7 (20...Rg7 21.Qa2+ d5 22.exd5 Qd6
[22...Kf8 23.d6] 23.Nd2 Bf5 24.Bc5 Qe5+ 25.Ne4 +-) **21.Rxh7 Kxh7**
22.Qf6! Nc6 23.Qf7+ Kh8 24.Qxg6 Qe7 25.Bd2 Black Resigns.

Game 41
Todorcevic-Georgadze
San Sebastian 1991

1.Nf3 c5 2.g3 Nc6 3.Bg2 g6 4.0-0 Bg7 5.e4 e6 6.d3 Nge7 7.c3 0-0
8.Re1 d6 9.a4 e5! 10.Na3 h6 (10...f5? 11.Qb3+ Kh8 12.Ng5) **11.Nc2**
Bg4!? 12.h3 Be6 13.d4 (13.b4 cxb4 14.cxb4 Bb3 15.Bd2 Rc8 threatening 16...Bxc2 and 17...Nxb4) **13...cxd4 14.cxd4 Bb3 15.Qd3** (15.dxe5

Nb4 16.exd6 Nxc2 17.dxe7 Qxe7 strongly favors Black) **15...Bxc2 16.Qxc2 Nxd4 17.Nxd4 exd4 18.Qd2 a5! 19.b4** (19.b3 Qb6 20.Rb1 Nc6) **19...axb4 20.Qxb4 Qd7 21.Bb2 Nc6 22.Qb5** (22.Qb3 Rfc8 with the idea Na5-c4) **22...Ra5 23.Qb3 Rfa8 24.f4 Nd8! 25.f5 g5** (25...gxf5 26.exf5 Rxf5 27.Qd3 is unclear) **26.Qf3 Bf6** (Much better than 26...Rxa4?! 27.f6 Bf8 28.Bxd4) **27.Qh5 Kg7 28.h4 Nc6 29.Bc1 Qe7 30.Qd1 Qe5 31.Ra3 b5 32.Qh5 Qe7 33.g4?** (Losing. The only way to resist was 33.e5 Nxe5 34.Bxa8 Rxa8 though Black would still be on top) **33...Ne5! 34.Rh3** (34.Rf1 d3!) **34...Rxa4 35.Rf1 Ra1! 36.Rb3**

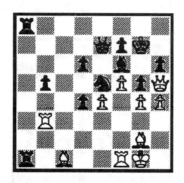

(After 36.hxg5 Bxg5 37.f6+ Qxf6! 38.Rxf6 Kxf6 the Bc1 falls and Black wins easily) **36...Rxc1!** (A fine Exchange sac which leaves White's Qh5 locked out of play) **37.Rxc1 gxh4 38.Rxb5 Bg5 39.Rf1 Kf6! 40.Rfb1 d3 41.Rb7 Ra1!** (After 42.Rxe7 Rxb1+ 43.Kf2 Kxe7 followed by Queening the d-pawn wins) **White Resigns.**

Game 42
Dzindzichashvili-Dvoretsky
Philadelphia 1991

1.e4 e6 2.d3 c5 3.Nf3 Nc6 4.g3 g6 5.Bg2 Bg7 6.0-0 Nge7 7.Re1 d6 8.c3 e5 9.a3 0-0 10.b4 h6 11.bxc5?! (11.Nbd2) **11...dxc5 12.c4 f5! 13.Nc3 f4** (=+) **14.Nd5 g5 15.h3 g4 16.Nh4! h5!** (Poor is 16...gxh3?! 17.Bf3 with the idea of Bg4) **17.Bb2 f3 18.Bf1 Qd6 19.Qd2!!** (With the

idea of Qg5) **19...Nxd5** (Not 19...Bh6?? 20.Nxe7+ Nxe7 21.Bxe5!)
20.exd5

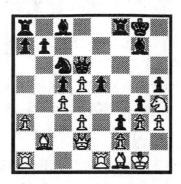

20...Bh6 21.Qxh6!! (On 21.Qc2 Nd4 22.Bxd4 exd4 and ...Bd7 gives
Black a clear advantage) **21...Qxh6 22.dxc6 Re8! 23.c7?!** (Correct was
23.cxb7 Bxb7 24.Rxe5 with murky play) **23...Qd6 24.Re3 Qxc7
25.Ng6??** (25.Rae1 Qb6! 26.Bxe5 Bd7 with clear advantage for Black,
but no immediate win) **25...Qb6! White Resigns.**

Game 43
Morozevich-Gulko
Intel Rapid Chess, Moscow 1995

    1.e4 e6 2.d3 c5 3.Nf3 Nc6 4.g3 (4 Nbd2!? g6? 5.c3 gives White the
advantage. Correct is 4...d5 5.Nbd2 g6 or 5...Bd6) **4...g6 5.Bg5 Qc7
6.Bg2 Bg7 7.c3 e5 8.0-0 d6 9.Na3 h6 10.Nb5 Qd7 11.Be3 Nge7 12.d4
Nxd4 13.Nbxd4 cxd4 14.cxd4 0-0 15.Qd2** (White has a clear advantage)
15...exd4

(see next diagram)

**16.Bxh6 Nc6 17.Bxg7 Kxg7 18.Nxd4 Qe7 19.Nxc6 bxc6 20.Rfd1 Rb8
21.b3 d5 22.exd5 cxd5 23.Qxd5 Qf6 24.Qd4 Qxd4 25.Rxd4 Re8
26.Re4 Rxe4 27.Bxe4 Rb4 28.Bf3 a5 29.Re1 Be6 30.Re4 Rb5 31.Be2
Rd5 32.Bc4 Rd1+ 33.Kg2 Bxc4 34.Rxc4 Rd2 35.Ra4 Rd5 36.Kf3 Kf6**

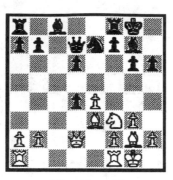

After 15...exd4

37.Ke3 g5 38.h4 gxh4 39.Rxh4 Kg5 40.Rd4 Rb5 41.Kd3 f5 42.Kc4 Re5 43.f4+ Black Resigns.

Game 44
Psakhis-Soffer
Bled 1995

1.e4 c5 2.Nf3 e6 3.d3 Nc6 4.g3 d5 5.Qe2 Nge7 6.Bg2 g6 7.0-0 Bg7 8.c3 b6 9.e5 Ba6 10.Re1 h6 11.h4 Nf5 12.Bf4 Qd7 13.Nbd2 Rc8 14.Nf1 Bb7 15.N1h2 Qe7 16.Ng4 Rd8 17.Qd2 Rh7 18.Rac1 Kf8 19.d4 c4 20.Bf1 Ke8 21.b3 Na5 22.b4 Nc6 23.Be2 Kd7 24.Bd1 Kc8 25.Bc2 Nb8 26.Kg2 Nd7 27.Rh1 h5 28.Ne3 Re8 29.Bg5 Qf8 30.Rce1 Kb8 31.Re2 Rc8 32.Rhe1 Bc6 33.Kg1 a6 34.Kf1 Ka7 35.Ng1 Rc7 36.Nh3 Bb7 37.Bd1 Ne7 38.Nf4 Qe8 39.Bc2 Rh8 40.Neg2 Rc8 41.Re3 Ng8 42.a4 Nh6 43.Kg1 Ng4 44.R3e2 Rc7 45.Qd1 Nh6 46.Nh3 Ng8 47.Ngf4 Nh6 48.Qb1 Nf8 49.Ng2 Ng8 50.b5 a5 51.f3 Nh6 52.Kf2 Nd7 53.Qc1 Bc8 54.Rg1 Qf8 55.Nhf4 Qe8 56.Nh3 Qf8 57.Ngf4 Qe8 58.Ke1 Nf5 59.Kd1 Rh7 60.Qd2 Qh8 61.Qe1 Bf8 62.Kc1 Bg7 63.Kb1 Bb7 64.Rh1

(see next diagram)

64...Nxe5 65.dxe5 d4 66.Bxf5 gxf5 67.cxd4 Bxf3 68.Rf1 Bxe2 69.Nxe2 Qf8 70.Qc3 Qa8 71.Nhf4 Bf8 72.Qf3 Qc8 73.Nc3 Bb4 74.Kc2 Rh8 75.Rd1 Rd7 76.Bf6 Rg8 77.Nxh5 Qf8 78.Bg5 Rc7 79.Nf6 Rh8 80.d5

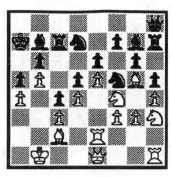

After 64.Rh1

Qa8 81.Qe3 Bc5 82.Qe2 exd5 83.Nfxd5 Rb7 84.h5 Qg8 85.Bf4 Qh7 86.Nf6 Qg7 87.Rd7 Rhb8 88.Rxb7+ Rxb7 89.h6 Qh8 90.h7 Bf8 91.Ncd5 Bg7 92.Qxc4 Qf8 93.Kb3 Qd8 94.Be3 Black Resigns.

Game 45
Kaidanov-Saidy
World Open 1995

1.e4 e6 2.d3 d5 3.Nd2 c5 4.g3 Nc6 5.Bg2 (A finesseful order of moves which rules out 5...Bd6 – the Karpov System, covered in Chapter 3) **5...Nge7 6.Ngf3 g6 7.0-0 Bg7 8.Re1 Qc7?** (Planning ...0-0-0; in Kaidanov-Zapata, New York 1993, 8...b6 was met by 9.c3 a5 [9...Ba6? 10.Qa4 Bxd3 11.exd5 b5 12.Qa6 wins] 10.a4 Ba6 11.exd5 Nxd5 12.Nc4 +=; if 9...Bb7 then 10.Qe2 Qc7 11.e5 followed by 12.Nf1) **9.exd5! exd5** (9...Nxd5 10.Nb3 b6 11.c4 Nde7 12.d4!, R.Byrne) **10.d4! cxd4** (10...c4 11.b3! [R.Byrne's 11.Nxc4!? dxc4 12.d5 0-0 13.d6 Qd7 14.dxe7 Re8 is unclear] 11...c3 12.Nb1 with the double threats 13.Nxc3 and 13.Ba3; e.g., 12...Bg4 13.Nxc3 Nxd4 14.Nxd5 wins, or if 11...b5 then 12.a4 is very strong) **11.Nb3 Bg4 12.Bf4 Qd8 13.h3 Bxf3 14.Qxf3 0-0 15.Rad1 h6 16.h4 b6 17.Bh3 a6 18.Nc1 Ra7 19.Nd3 Re8 20.Be5! Nf5** (20...Bxe5 21.Nxe5 f5 22.h5!. R.Byrne) **21.Bxg7 Nxg7 22.Nf4 Ne5 23.Qb3 d3 24.Kf1! dxc2 25.Rxd5 Qc7 26.Rc1 Qc4 27.Qxc4 Nxc4 28.Rxc2 b5 29.b3 Nb6 30.Rd6 Rb8 31.h5! g5 32.Nd3 Nxh5**

33.Rcc6 Na8 34.Rxh6 Ng7 35.Rxa6 Rxa6 36.Rxa6 Nc7 37.Ra7 Nge6 38.Ne5 Ra8 39.Rxa8 Nxa8 40.Bxe6 fxe6 41.Nf3 g4 42.Ne5 Nb6 43.Nxg4 Nd5 44.a4 bxa4 45.bxa4 Kf7 46.Ne3 Nc3 47.a5 Ke7 48.a6 Nb5 49.Ke2 Kd7 50.Kd3 Nc7 51.a7 Kc6 52.Ke4 Kb6 53.Ke5 Kxa7 54.g4 Kb7 55.g5 Black Resigns.

CHAPTER TWO

The Keres System

Game 46
Yermolinsky-Berry
Washington State Open 1994

1.Nf3 d5 2.g3 Nf6 3.Bg2 c6 4.0-0 Bg4 (The Keres System is one of the most solid defenses to the KIA. Black pawns on d5 and c6 create a bulwark to limit the activity of the Bg2. The Black QB is brought out early to g4, anticipating e2-e4, after which there is a pin on White's Nf3. In some cases, after White "puts the question" to the Bg4 by h3, Black will trade off with ...Bxf3, leaving White with fewer pieces and consequently less chance of mounting large scale pressure against the solid Black game. On the other hand, this surrender of the Bishop pair can be used to maintain slight but persistent positional pressure in some cases. Hence, often Black answers h3 with the circumspect retreat ...Bh5, retaining the two Bishops and the pin on the Nf3. But then White can choose the peculiar-looking Queen shift Qe1, unpinning and reinforcing the e4-pawn as preparation [in case of ...dxe4 and dxe4] for Nd2-c4. After White's e2-e4, it is often advisable for Black to trade ...dxe4, as after White's dxe4 the resulting fixed central pawn structure hinders the action of the Bg2. Also, this early pawn trade prevents the possibility of exd5 followed by c2-c4. See Game 50 for this scenario) **5.d3 Nbd7 6.Nbd2 e5 7.h3 Bh5 8.e4 dxe4** (Black astutely makes the aforementioned pawn trade to try to dampen White's potential) **9.dxe4 Qc7 10.Qe1 Bxf3 11.Nxf3 Be7** (Another point of 10.Qe1 arises after 11...Bc5 when 12.b4! gains space and time) **12.Nh4!** (f5 beckons to the Knight) **12...g6?!**

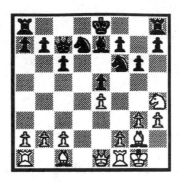

(This "cure" is worse than the disease. Simply 12...0-0 would leave White only a little better) **13.Bh6!** (Of course! Now Black's uncastled King will be the source of difficulties) **13...Nh5 14.Nf3 Qb6?!** (Threatening 15...Nxg3 16.Be3 Bc5; but this is effortlessly met, so the net result is loss of time) **15.Kh1 Qxb2?** (A suicidal pawn grab) **16.Rb1 Qxc2 17.Rxb7** (This monster on the 7th more than compensates for the pawn) **17...f6 18.Qc1!** (Well done! White realizes that he has decisive pressure even with the Queens off, as his Rooks will show devastating activity) **18...Qxc1 19.Rxc1 Rb8 20.Rxa7 Rb2 21.Be3 Nb8 22.Nd2 Ng7 23.Nc4 Rb4** (After 23...Rb5 24.Bf1 is very strong, but the text is immediately fatal) **24.Rxe7+ Black Resigns.**

Game 47
Botvinnik-Szilagyi
Amsterdam 1966

1.g3 (Indicating a willingness to play a Pirc/Modern Defense [with colors reversed] if Black plays 1...e5 followed by ...d5, etc) **1...d5 2.Nf3 c6 3.Bg2 Bg4 4.d3 Nd7 5.h3 Bxf3** (Playable, but we feel the immediate surrender of the Bishop pair is less flexible than 5...Bh5) **6.Bxf3 e5** (More solid is 6...e6 to muffle the action of the Bf3) **7.Nd2 Ngf6 8.e4** (Worth considering is 8.0-0 followed by c4, trying to press on the h1-a8 diagonal) **8...dxe4 9.dxe4** (Keeping the long diagonal open with 9.Nxe4 is quite possible, but the simplification 9...Nxe4 10.Bxe4 probably didn't appeal to Botvinnik, who liked heavy-caliber positional struggles) **9...Bc5 10.0-0 Qe7 11.c3 0-0?!**

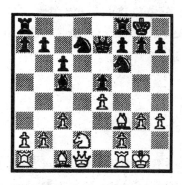

(This "automatic" move is a significant positional error, allowing White to gain space and time with the following thrust. Correct was the restraining move 11...a5) **12.b4! Bb6 13.a4** (Grabbing more space and holding the option of a5 for a favorable moment) **13...Rfd8 14.Qc2 Rac8 15.Be2!** (Botvinnik realizes the KB has a future on c4 and so avoids the stereotyped 15.Bg2) **15...c5??** (An awful positional blunder, shutting in his Bishop while giving White a strong square for his pieces at c4) **16.b5 Ne8 17.Nc4 Nd6 18.Bg5!** (A nice finesse designed to induce the weakening of the a2-g8 diagonal. Now if 18...Qxg5 then 19.Nxd6 Rb8 [19...Rc7?? 20.a5] 20.Bc4 Rf8 21.Rfd1 threatening 22.Nxf7 is very strong) **18...f6 19.Be3 Nxc4 20.Bxc4+** (Verifying the logic of 15.Be2!) **20...Kh8 21.a5 Bc7 22.Rfd1 Nf8** (Notice that neither of Black's minor pieces has a good post) **23.Qa2!** (Emphasizing Black's low mobility; now even ...Ne6 is not allowed, while the push a5-a6 is at hand) **23...Rxd1+ 24.Rxd1 Rd8 25.Rxd8!** (Botvinnik doesn't fear simplification as his remaining forces are far superior to Black's) **25...Bxd8 26.a6** (Now White's Queen is freed from guarding the a-pawn; also, the a6 pawn can become a menace – see note to Black's 31st) **26...b6 27.Kg2 Qd7 28.Qe2!** (Excellently conceived. Botvinnik wants to place his Queen in front of his Bishop to invade along the a2-g8 diagonal) **28...Ng6 29.Bb3! Ne7 30.Qc4 h6 31.Qf7!** Kh7 (The value of having the pawn on a6 is shown in the line 31...Qxb5 32.Qf8+ Kh7 33.Qxd8 Qxb3 34.Qxe7 Qc4 35.Qxa7 Qxe4+ 36.Kh2 f5 37.Qb7 and the a-pawn waltzes in to Queen) **32.Bc4 Qd6 33.h4!** (With the idea of h5/Qe8/Bf7 and Bg6+) **33...Qd1 34.Qe8 f5 35.exf5 Nxf5 36.Bg8+ Kh8** (Now after 37.Bf7+ Kh7 38.Bg6#) **Black Resigns.**

Game 48
Chernov-Neverov
Ukrainian Championship 1991

   1.Nf3 d5 2.g3 c6 3.Bg2 Nf6 4.0-0 Bg4 5.d3 Nbd7 6.Nbd2 e5 7.h3 Bh5 8.Nh4 (With the idea of obtaining the Bishop pair after g4 and Nxg6; also, Nf5 is another possibility) **8...Bc5** (On 8...Bd6 9.Nf5 is quite annoying) **9.c3 0-0 10.b4!** (Gaining space and time) **10...Bb6 11.c4** (Very good. White realizes that this way of striking at the Black center is more promising in the given position than playing for the "usual" e2-e4) **11...Re8 12.g4 Bd4!?** (After 12...Bg6 13.Nxg6 hxg6 14.e3! White has a nice compact center and a very active Bg2 – a small but clear positional advantage. With the text, Black tries to avoid this scenario by "mixing it up." But as we shall see, White's position is quite resilient)

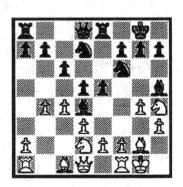

13.Rb1 Nxg4 14.hxg4 Qxh4 15.gxh5 e4 (Preventing the defensive resource Nf3 and threatening 16...e3) **16.dxe4!** (Envisaging later use of the third rank to quell Black's attacking play) **16...dxe4 17.Nxe4 Rxe4 18.Bxe4 Qxe4 19.Rb3 Qg4+ 20.Kh1** (Not 20.Rg3?? Qxg3+) **20...Nf6**

(20...Qxh5+ 21.Kg2 Qg4+ 22.Rg3 wins for White) **21.Rg3 Qxh5+ 22.Kg2 Qe5 23.Rg5!** (This Rook has almost single-handedly repulsed Black's attack) **23...Qe4+?** (This loses directly, but even after 23...Qd6 24.e3 Be5 25.Qxd6 Bxd6 26.Bb2 White dominates) **24.f3 Qh4 25.e4!** (Threatening 26.Qxd4 while encircling the Black Queen) **25...Rd8 26.Qe2 Be5 27.f4** (27.Rxe5) **Black Resigns.**

Game 49
Ubilava-Castellano
Las Palmas 1994

1.Nf3 d5 2.g3 Bg4 3.Bg2 c6 4.d3 Nd7 5.Nbd2 Ngf6 6.h3 Bxf3 (This early surrender of the two Bishops gives White a slight pull. More patient is 6...Bh5) **7.Nxf3 e6** (Black avoids 7...e5 as he intends to reinforce d5 to the maximum to reduce the scope of the Bg2) **8.0-0 Be7 9.c3 0-0 10.Qc2** (Preparing e4) **10...a5 11.e4 dxe4 12.dxe4 a4?!** (Better was 12...e5 to stop White's next)

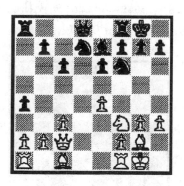

13.e5 (Now White has control of both e5 and e4, excellent preconditions for pressure on the center and Kingside) **13...Nd5 14.Re1 Qc7 15.h4 h6 16.Bd2 Rfd8 17.Rad1 Ra5 18.a3 Raa8** (Obviously Black doesn't have a good plan) **19.Bf1!** (The KB seeks greener pastures) **19...N5b6 20.g4!** (Very strong. Now a breakthrough by h5 and g5 is in the air) **20...Nf8 21.h5 Nbd7 22.Bf4 Ra5 23.Bc4 f6** (Black tries to break the bind, but this only plays into White's hands) **24.Qe4 Nxe5 25.Bxe5** (Not 25.Nxe5

Rxd1 26.Rxd1 fxe5) **25...fxe5 26.Rxd8 Bxd8 27.Nxe5 Bf6 28.Ng6!**
(Knocking out the defense of e6) **28...Qd7 29.Nxf8 Kxf8 30.Bxe6
Qd2 31.Re2 Qd1+ 32.Kg2 Re5 33.Qb4+ Ke8 34.Qxb7! Rxe2**
(34...Qxe2 allows 35.Qf7+ Kd8 36.Qd7#, but the text merely prolongs
the inevitable) **35.Qf7+ Kd8 36.Qf8+ Kc7 37.Qc8+ Kb6** (37...Kd6
drops the Queen after 38.Qd7+) **38.Qb8+** (But now 38...Kc5 39.Qb4#
or 38...Ka6 39.Bc8+ Ka5 40.Qb4#) **Black Resigns.**

Game 50
Vaganian-Torre
Moscow Olympiad 1994

    **1.Nf3 d5 2.g3 c6 3.Bg2 Bg4 4.d3 Nd7 5.0-0 Ngf6 6.Nbd2 e5 7.e4
Bd6** (Black feels happy; all of his minor pieces are developed and he has
a "classical" two pawn center. But this happy view is not all there is to
the position. As we will see White has in mind a vigorous counterattack
against this proud pawn center) **8.h3 Bh5 9.exd5!** (The "fly in the
ointment." Now Black's classical center will be the object of hypermodern vengeance) **9...cxd5** (Not 9...Nxd5 10.Nc4) **10.c4!**

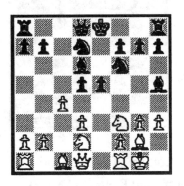

(White has cleverly turned the position into a sort of Benoni – with an
extra tempo that fully justifies a driving initiative) **10...0-0** (To be
considered is 10...d4) **11.cxd5 Nxd5 12.Qb3** (A fine, aggressive post for
the Queen which emphasizes the absence of Black's QB from the
Queenside) **12...N5f6 13.Nc4** (Unproductive would be 13.Qxb7 Nc5

14.Qb5 Rb8 15.Qc4 Bg6 16.Ne1 [16.Nxe5 Bxe5 17.Qxc5 Bd4 18.Qc2 Bxd3!] 16...Rc8 with excellent play for Black) **13...Bc7** (For 13...Nc5 see the next game) **14.Be3** (Preventing 14...Nc5) **14...b6 15.Rfe1** (Notice White's very active, well-coordinated pieces in play against Black's center [what's left of it!] and Queenside) **15...Rc8 16.d4!** (Opening up lines for his better placed pieces) **16...Bxf3** (It's no fun to give up the two Bishops in an open position, but 16...exd4 17.Nxd4 is very strong for White) **17.Bxf3 e4** (Desperately trying to keep the terrible Bishop bottled-up) **18.Bg2 Re8 19.Rac1 h6** (The attempt to use the d5 square in front of White's isolated d-pawn fails: 19...Nd5 20.Nd6! Bxd6 21.Rxc8 Qxc8 22.Qxd5 with White dominating) **20.Qb5!** (Invading the weakened light-squares) **20...Bb8 21.a4** (With ideas of a5) **21...Bc7 22.Red1 Bb8 23.b4!** (Gaining still more space, a classic "positional squeeze" stratagem) **23...Qe7 24.a5 bxa5** (24...Bc7 25.d5!) **25.bxa5 Qe6 26.d5** (White's space control in the center and Queenside is simply awesome) **26...Qf5 27.g4! Qg6 28.d6 Rcd8 29.a6 Re6 30.Qf5!** (White realizes that an ending is hopeless for Black) **30...Qxf5 31.gxf5 Ree8 32.Na5!** (Threatening 33.Nc6 Rc8 34.Ne7+) **32...Ne5 33.Nb7 Rc8 34.Rxc8 Rxc8 35.Bd4! Ned7** (35...Nfd7 36.Bxe5 Nxe5 37.d7 wins) **36.Bxf6 gxf6 37.Bxe4 Kg7 38.Bd3 Rc6 39.Bf1 h5 40.Rd5** (40.Bb5 wins material; but White was probably in time pressure and just wanted "any move" to make the time control) **Black Resigns.**

Game 51
Vaganian-Kaidanov
USA 1994

1.Nf3 d5 2.g3 c6 3.Bg2 Bg4 4.0-0 Nd7 5.d3 Ngf6 6.Nbd2 e5 7.e4 Bd6 (Perhaps the best route here is 7...dxe4 8.dxe4 Be7, but Black wanted a more dynamic set-up. For 7...Be7, see the next game) **8.h3 Bh5 9.exd5! cxd5 10.c4! 0-0 11.cxd5 Nxd5 12.Qb3 N5f6 13.Nc4 Nc5** (Varying from 13...Bc7, seen in the previous game) **14.Qa3!**

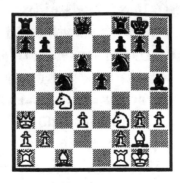

14...Bxf3 (Due to the pressure on e5, Black has to give up the Bishop pair) **15.Bxf3 Be7 16.Nxe5 Ncd7** (Black hopes to find compensation for the pawn by quick development while harassing White's Queen) **17.Qc3 Rc8 18.Qe1** (Poor is 18.Qd4? Bc5 19.Qf4 Nxe5 20.Qxe5 Qxd3 21.Bxb7 Bd4! 22.Qg5 h6 23.Qf4 Rc2 with strong counterplay) **18...Bc5 19.Nxd7 Qxd7 20.Kg2** (It's now becoming clear that Black doesn't have enough for the pawn) **20...b6 21.Bg5! Qf5** (21...Qxd3 22.Bxf6 gxf6 and Black's Kingside pawns are shattered) **22.Qd2 Bd4 23.Be3 Rcd8 24.Rad1** (White consolidates while Black hopes to build counterplay along the d-file) **24...Rd7 25.Rfe1 Rfd8 26.Bf4 Nd5 27.Bg5** (Not 27.Bg4? Nxf4+ 28.gxf4 Qd5+) **27...Nf6 28.Re2 h6 29.Bxf6 Bxf6** (Though Black has "achieved" opposite-colored Bishops, White still has slight chances to score the point. However, it will require patience and excellent technique) **30.Rde1 Qb5** (Not 30...Rxd3? 31.Re8+ Kh7 32.Qxd3! Rxd3 33.Be4, or 30...Qxd3? 31.Qxd3 Rxd3 32.Re8+ Rxe8 33.Rxe8+ Kh7 34.Be4+) **31.Qc2 Qc5 32.Qa4** (Not 32.Qxc5? bxc5 and White's winning chances are nil) **32...g6 33.Rc2 Qd4 34.Qxd4 Rxd4 35.Be4** (Finally the d-pawn is securely protected, but it is difficult to make progress) **35...Bg7 36.g4 Bf8 37.f4 Bc5 38.Rf1 Kg7 39.f5 R4d6 40.Kf3 R8d7 41.Ke2 Rd8 42.Rfc1 R8d7 43.b3 Rd8 44.Rc4 Rd4 45.fxg6 fxg6 46.Rxc5!?** (By sacrificing the Rook for Bishop and pawn, White eliminates the opposite-colored Bishops in a new bid for the win, but Black should be able to hold the draw with accurate play) **46...bxc5 47.Rxc5 R8d7 48.Ke3**

R4d6 49.Ra5 Re7?! 50.b4 Rde6 51.Kd4 Rd7+ 52.Kc4 Kf6?! (52...Rde7!) 53.a4 Rc7+ 54.Kb3 Ke7 55.Rb5 Kd8 56.a5 Rc1 57.g5 hxg5 58.Rxg5 Ke7 59.h4 Rb1+ 60.Kc3 Rc1+ 61.Kb2 Re1 62.Bxg6 R6e2+ 63.Kc3 Rc1+ 64.Kd4 Rb2 65.Rb5 Rcb1 66.Kc3 Rh2 67.Rb7+ Kd6 68.Rxa7 Rxh4 69.Be4 Rh2 70.Rb7 Ke5 71.Rb5+ Kd6 72.Kd4 Ra1 73.Rg5 Kc7 74.Kc5 Rc2+ 75.Kb5 Rb2 76.a6 Rab1 77.Rc5+ Kd6 78.Rc4 Ra1 79.Kb6 Black Resigns.

Game 52
Vaganian-Kaidanov
USA 1994

1.Nf3 d5 2.g3 c6 3.Bg2 Bg4 4.0-0 Nd7 5.d3 Ngf6 6.Nbd2 e5 7.e4 **Be7** (A modest but secure location for this Bishop. For 7...Bd6 see the previous game) **8.h3 Bh5 9.Qe1 Qc7 10.Nh4** (The occupation of f5 with a Knight is a recurring positional theme in this type of pawn structure) **10...0-0 11.Nf5 Bc5 12.Nb3**

(Notice how White operates with "little threats" against the Bishop. This is typical of the "creeping" nature of KIA stratagems) **12...Bb6 13.a4 a5** (To stop a5, but now the a5-pawn is subject to pressure) **14.Be3 Rfe8 15.Kh1 dxe4** (Strategically incorrect would be 15...d4?! as after 16.Bc1! [leaving d2 for the Nb3] followed by f4, White has fine prospects on the Kingside, while Black's pieces would be inappropriately placed for meaningful counterplay) **16.dxe4 Bg6 17.Bxb6 Nxb6 18.Nh4!** (Astutely played. The obvious 18.Nxa5 would allow Black counterplay by 18...Bxf5! 19.exf5 e4. The trade ...Bxf5 followed by ...e4 should be closely watched in such positions) **18...Nc4 19.Qc3 b5** (Black tries to hold his own by anchoring this Knight on c4. But White will soon show that the "anchor" can be loosened) **20.Rfe1 Qb6 21.Kg1 Red8 22.Nxg6! hxg6 23.Bf1!** (White's last two moves prepare an attack on c4) **23...Qa6 24.Kg2** (After 24.Bxc4 bxc4 25.Nd2 Black holds with 25...Rd4) **24...Nd7 25.Red1** (Threatening 26.Rxd7! Rxd7 27.Nc5 Qa7 28.Nxd7 Qxd7 29.Bxc4 winning a pawn) **25...Ndb6 26.Nc5 Qc8 27.b3** (Finally ousting Black's c4 outpost. Note that White's c5 outpost is safe from pawn attacks) **27...b4 28.Qe1 Na3?** (A poor post for the Knight. Better was the natural 28...Nd6, though White retains the advantage by 29.Rd3! intending to stack his heavy pieces on the d-file) **29.Rac1 Rxd1 30.Qxd1 Qf8 31.Nd3 Rd8 32.c3!** (Opening up lines to invade and attack Black's Queenside) **32...c5 33.cxb4 cxb4 34.Rc6 Rd6 35.Qc1 f6 36.Qc5! Rxc6 37.Qxc6 Qd8 38.Nc5 Nb1** (Trying to get back into play, but it is far too late) **39.Ne6 Qb8 40.Ba6!** (Now if 40...Nd2 then 41.Bb7! Qa7 42.Qc7 mates) **40...Qa8 41.Qc7 Black Resigns.**

Game 53
Korchnoi-Flear
Lugano 1992

1.Nf3 d5 2.g3 Nf6 3.Bg2 c6 4.0-0 Bg4 5.d3 e6 6.Qe1! (This bizarre-looking Queen move has become a routine method in this and similar KIA positions. It supports e4 while ducking the pin on the d1-h5 diagonal. The natural 6.Re1 is possible, but White would rather have this Rook left on the Kingside where it might help with a later Kingside attack) **6...Nbd7 7.e4 dxe4 8.dxe4 e5 9.Nbd2 Bc5** (On c5 the Bishop can be harassed by Nb3 or b2-b4; hence 9...Be7 seems more prudent) **10.Nc4 Qe7?!** (On e7 the Queen is exposed to the possibility of a later Nf5. Correct was 10...Bxf3 11.Bxf3 Qe7 12.Ne3 g6! with equal chances) **11.Ne3 h5?** (Since on 11...Bh5 12.Nf5 follows, Black tries to play aggressively. But aggressive play in a slightly inferior position is bound to fail. Relatively best was 11...Bxe3, after which White's two Bishops confer a slight, yet long-term positional plus) **12.a3!** (Korchnoi realizes that after 11...h5?, Kingside castling is out of the question; so he prepares to "greet" the Black King after he castles long) **12...0-0-0 13.b4 Bd6 14.Nh4** (Threatening Nf5 and inducing the following weakening) **14...g6 15.c4 Nh7 16.h3 Be6 17.Qc3 Kb8 18.Rd1 Bc7**

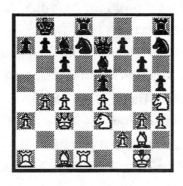

(Now, instead of the actually played 19.Bb2, very interesting is the shot 19.Nd5!! with great complications, e.g. 19...cxd5 20.exd5 and now a: 20...e4?! 21.d6!! Bxd6 22.Rxd6, with a1: 22...g5!? 23.Qd4!! gxh4 [if 23...Ndf6, then 23.Bxg5! Rxd6 24.Bf4 Rhd8 25.c5 with White on top, or if 23...Nxg5 24.Rxd8+ followed by 25.Qe5+ and 26.Qxg5.] 24.Bf4! Ka8 [Or if 24...Kc8 then 25.Qxa7 threatens 26.Rc6+!.] 25.Ra6!! Nc5 26.Qxc5 Qxc5 27.bxc5 and now if 27...bxa6 then 28.Bxe4+ wins. Or 27...hxg3 28.fxg3 Bxc4 29.Ra4 and White's game is clearly better; a2: 22...Nb6 23.Rxd8+ Rxd8 24.Qxe4! with the idea of Nf5. Next is b: 20...Ndf6!? 21.Be3 g5 [on 21...Bc8 22.c5] 22.Bc5! Bd6 [or 22...Qe8 23.d6! Bb6 24.Qxe5 with the threat 25.d7+.] 23.Bxd6+ Qxd6 [23...Rxd6 24.Qxe5!] 24.dxe6! Qxd1+ 25.Rxd1 Rxd1+ 26.Kh2 gxh4 27.Qxe5+ Ka8 [27...Kc8 28.Qc5+ wins.] 28.Qc7 hxg3+ 29.fxg3 Rb8 30.c5! fxe6 31.c6 [hoping for 31...b6 32.Qxh7! Nxh7 33.c7+ Rb7 34.c8=Q#] 31...Nd5 32.cxb7+ Rxb7 33.Qc8+ Rb8 34.Qxe6 Rd8 35.Qe2! Rd4 36.Qf2 Rc4 [36...Rd3 or 37...Rd1 is strongly met by 37.Qc2] 37.Qf5 Rd4 38.Qxh7 will win for White. Finally, c: 20...Bf5 21.c5 followed by d6 gives White good chances.) **19.Bb2 Ng5 20.Kh2 Nf6 21.Qc2 Bc8** (To be considered was simplification by 21...Rxd1, though White would still have a small plus) **22.b5 Ne6** (Or 22...c5 23.Nd5 Nxd5 24.cxd5 with advantage for White) **23.bxc6 Nd4!?** (Black refuses to go down without a fight, but perhaps better was 23...bxc6! 24.Rab1 Ka8 25.Qa4 Nc5! with unclear play) **24.Bxd4 exd4 25.cxb7 Bxh3!?** (After 25...dxe3 26.bxc8=Q+ Kxc8 27.f4 White has a terrific position) **26.Nd5! Nxd5 27.cxd5 Bg4** (On 27...Qxh4 28.Qxc7+! Kxc7 29.gxh4 Bxg2 30.Kxg2 Kxb7 31.Rxd4 White's central pawn duo gives him a winning endgame) **28.Kg1!** (A fine Exchange offer which Black should have refused) **28...Bxd1?** (Now White will be in control. The only way to mix it up was 28...g5!?. For example, a: 29.Nf3 Bxf3 30.Bxf3 g4 31.Bg2 h4 32.gxh4 Qxh4 33.Rxd4 Bb6 34.Rad1 g3 with strong threats for Black [the best chance for White was 33.Kf1!? g3 34.Rd3!], or b: 29.Nf5 Bxf5 30.exf5 h4 31.g4 h3 32.Bf3 with unclear play and chances for both sides) **29.Rxd1 Qxa3 30.Nf3 Qc3 31.Qb1 Bb6** (Otherwise White plays Nxd4 and Nc6+) **32.Ne5 Rd6 33.Rc1!** (The sharpest way, though 33.Nxf7 is also good. White feels his Knight is worth more than a Rook) **33...Qa3 34.Nc4 Qc5 35.e5! Rdd8** (Or 35...Rxd5 36.Nxb6 Qxb6 37.Qxb6 axb6 38.Bxd5) **36.Nd6!** (Protecting the b7-pawn and preparing a tactical penetration down the c-file) **36...Qa3 37.Qc2** (Threatening 38.Qc8+! Rxc8 39.Rxc8+ Rxc8 40.bxc8=Q#. If 37...a6 then 38.Qc8+! still mates by force: 38...Rxc8 39.Rxc8+ Rxc8 40.bxc8=Q+ Ka7 41.Qb7#) **Black Resigns.**

Game 54
Hickl-Masserey
Horgen 1994

1.g3 d5 2.Nf3 Nf6 3.Bg2 c6 4.b3 (This double-fianchetto is another basic strategic option in the KIA) **4...Bg4 5.Bb2 Nbd7 6.d3 e6 7.Nbd2 Bd6 8.0-0 0-0 9.c4** (A good example of a flexible outlook on opening play. While it is true the traditional method of play in the KIA involves playing for e4 at some point [e.g., 9.Qe1 and e4], it is quite possible to switch into an English-Reti structure with c4. We give this example for those who wish to try this course) **9...Re8 10.Qc2 a5 11.a3 e5 12.e4** (To stop 12...e4 and ...e3) **12...dxe4 13.dxe4 Bf8 14.Bc3!**

(To advance b4 followed by c5 and Nc4 with strong pressure against Black's center and Queenside) **14...Qc7 15.b4 axb4 16.axb4 Rxa1 17.Rxa1 Nb8?** (This looks rather fatalistic. He should have tried 17...c5 to stop 18.c5) **18.c5 Nfd7 19.Nc4 f6 20.Ra7** (The b7-pawn is now a serious weakness) **20...Qc8 21.Nfd2 Be6 22.Bf1 Kh8 23.Qb1** (On 23.Qa2 Black could play 23...b5) **23...Be7 24.Qa1 Rd8 25.Na5 b6 26.cxb6** (Threatening 27.Rc7; if 26...Nxb6 27.Rxe7) **Black Resigns.**

Game 55
Dzindzichashvili-Qi Kinghuan
Thessaloniki Olympiad 1984

1.Nf3 d5 2.g3 c6 3.Bg2 Bg4 4.0-0 Nd7 5.d3 e5 6.e4 dxe4 7.dxe4 Bc5 (As seen in previous games, this Bishop is often exposed on c5; so 7...Be7 seems preferable) **8.h3 Bh5 9.Nbd2 f6?!** (Black feels the Bh5 needs to be brought onto the a2-g8 diagonal, but the weakening effect of 9...f6?! exceeds any benefit) **10.c3 Bf7 11.Nh4!**

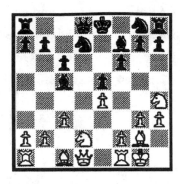

(Taking advantage of the gratuitous unpinning of the Nf3, the horse heads for f5) **11...Ne7 12.Nf5 Nxf5 13.exf5** (While Black has removed the f5 outpost, now the e4-square will soon prove to be a fine base for the QN) **13...Be7 14.Ne4 Nc5 15.Qg4!** (Probing Black's Kingside. Now 15...0-0 fails to 16.Bh6) **15...g5 16.Be3 Nxe4** (Eliminating the "other" troublesome steed, but the KB on e4 proves to be an unpleasant visitor as well) **17.Bxe4 Qc7 18.Rfd1 h5** (Trying to find some play. But the passive position of his Bishops plus his awkwardly posted King ensure White's advantage) **19.Qe2 h4 20.Kg2 Kf8 21.Rd2 Rd8 22.Rxd8+ Bxd8 23.Rd1!** (Now if 23...Bxa2 24.Qd3! Be7 25.c4 leaves the Ba2 in the lurch) **23...Be7 24.Qd3 Qb8 25.Qc2** (White's Bishops rake the Queenside. Soon Black will have to move a pawn there to defend, which in turn will create further square weaknesses – allowing White to increase the bind) **25...a6** (Anticipating Qa4, but now b6 is permanently weakened) **26.Bb6 Qc8 27.c4 Be8 28.Qd2 hxg3 29.fxg3 Kg7 30.g4 Rh7 31.Qa5 Bd7 32.Bc5!** (The trade of Bishops will allow White to invade on d6) **32...Kf8 33.Bxe7+ Rxe7 34.Rd6 Kf7 35.Qd2 Qc7 36.h4!** (The decisive breakthrough) **36...gxh4 37.g5 fxg5 38.f6 Bh3+ 39.Kxh3 Qc8+ 40.Kh2 Qg4 41.Bg6+! Kxg6 42.fxe7+ Black Resigns.**

Game 56
Vaganian-Lau
Germany 1991

1.Nf3 d5 2.g3 c6 3.Bg2 Bg4 4.0-0 Nd7 5.d3 e6 6.b3 Be7?! (Intending to challenge control of the a1-h8 diagonal by ...Bf6; but this procedure seems artificial) **7.Bb2 Bf6 8.d4! h5?!**

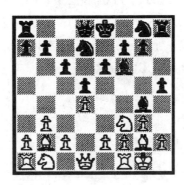

(Another point of the KB's development is revealed – an attack based on the early advance of the h-pawn. But White's position is perfectly sound; this premature flank attack will be punished in the classic manner – by a central counterattack) **9.Nbd2 h4 10.e4 hxg3 11.hxg3 Bg5** (Another artificial move, but this is a logical consequence of earlier indiscretions) **12.Qe1 Bxd2** (On 12...Qf6 13.Ne5! [a centralized reaction] is strong. However, now the advantage of the two Bishops is on White's side) **13.Nxd2 Ne7** (13...Qg5 is met by 14.f4! Qh6 15.Kf2 Ngf6 16.Rh1 with advantage for White) **14.c4** (Threatening to win material by trading on d5; the central counterattack is in full swing) **14...Nf6 15.Qe3 Bh5 16.Rfe1 Bg6 17.Rad1** (All of White's forces are massed in the center – an ominous sign for Black) **17...Qb6 18.Ba3** (Stopping Black from castling, while threatening 19.Bxe7 followed by captures on d5) **18...Rd8 19.Qc3 Rd7 20.Bc5 Qd8 21.e5** (Switching to a policy of constriction) **21...Nfg8 22.a4!** (Typical constriction policy: Black's position is totally passive, so White simply gains more and more space.

Then maneuvering with his pieces will precede a decisive breakthrough) **22...Nh6 23.a5! a6** (Otherwise 24.Bxa7) **24.Bb6 Qa8 25.Nf3!** (Intending the strong maneuver Ng5-h3-f4) **25...0-0** (After 25...Be4 26.Ng5 Bxg2 27.Kxg2 followed by Rh1 is strong) **26.Ng5 Re8 27.Nh3 Qb8 28.Nf4 Bf5 29.Bf3 Nc8 30.Bc5 Qc7 31.Kg2** (Ironically, White will now use the h-file) **31...Qd8 32.Rh1 f6** (Forced, otherwise White simply piles up on the h-file [Rh5/Rah1] and arranges for g4-g5) **33.Bh5 Nf7 34.g4 Be4+ 35.f3 Bh7 36.Ng6** (Black is in "semi-Zugzwang") **36...Ng5 37.Rde1 dxc4** (Possibly in time pressure, Black self-destructs) **38.bxc4 b6 39.axb6 Nxb6 40.Ra1 Black Resigns.**

Game 57
Damljanovic-Hansen
New York 1987

1.g3 d5 2.Nf3 Nf6 3.Bg2 c6 4.0-0 Bg4 5.d3 Nbd7 6.Nbd2 e5 7.h3 Bh5 8.e4 dxe4 9.dxe4 Bc5 (More solid is 9...Be7) **10.Qe1 Bxf3** (Giving up the Bishop pair in order to simplify and gain slightly more control of the dark-squares. Since Knights are by nature capable of controlling not only light but dark-squares, eliminating "half" of White's horses enhances Black's dark-squared control) **11.Bxf3 0-0 12.a4** (Staking out territory on the Queenside, a typical KIA stratagem) **12...Qe7 13.Qe2 a5 14.Nc4 Ne8** (Dark-squared strategy. The Knight is heading for e6) **15.Bd2** (A finesse, inducing a slight weakening of Black's Queenside) **15...b6**

(see next diagram)

16.Bg4! (Activating the KB) **16...Nc7 17.Kg2** (Not 17.Bxd7 Qxd7 18.Nxe5 Qxh3 threatening 19...Qxg3+) **17...Ne6 18.c3** (Black's dark-squared strategy seems ineffective as the Ne6's scope is curtailed by the c3 and g3 pawns) **18...g6?!** (Weakening and allowing the following incursion. Possibly Black intended to play ...h5 next but forgot about Bh6) **19.Bh6** (Of course!) **19...Rfe8 20.h4!** (Probing Black's Kingside

After 15...b6

and thus slightly increasing the strategic pressure) **20...f6 21.Rad1 Ndf8 22.h5 Rad8 23.Bc1 Rxd1 24.Rxd1 Rd8 25.Rh1** (Naturally White avoids exchanges) **25...Qd7 26.Qf3 Qd3** (Seeking safety in the endgame, but White's two Bishops and slightly better pawn structure give enduring pressure) **27.Qxd3 Rxd3 28.Kf1 Rd8 29.Ke2 Kf7 30.f3 Ng7 31.h6!** (A nice constricting move. Also, there is the long-term chance of attacking the fixed h7-pawn by Bg8. See White's 43rd move) **31...Ne8 32.Be3!** (The trade of Bishops fingers the weakness of b6) **32...Bxe3 33.Kxe3 Nd6** (33...Rb8? is too passive) **34.Nxd6+** (Not 34.Nxb6 Rb8) **34...Rxd6 35.b4!** (Threatening 36.bxa5 bxa5 37.Rb1 with penetration on the b-file) **35...axb4 36.cxb4** (But now White will have an outside passer with a4-a5) **36...Rd4 37.Rb1 Ke7 38.a5 b5 39.f4 Nd7 40.Rb3!** (Threatening to trade off the Rooks by Rd3 with a winning B vs. N ending) **40...Nb8 41.Bc8 Kd8 42.Be6!** (The h7-pawn is doomed) **42...Na6 43.Bg8 Nxb4 44.Bxh7 Nc2+ 45.Kf2 Rd2+ 46.Kg1 Rd1+ 47.Kg2 Rd2+ 48.Kh3 Kc7 49.fxe5 fxe5 50.Rb2 Rd7 51.Bg8 Nd4 52.h7 Rxh7+** ("Better" was resigning) **53.Bxh7 c5 54.Bxg6 c4 55.Bf7 c3 56.Rb1 Kb7 57.g4 Black Resigns.**

Game 58
Kogan-Seirawan
USA 1985

1.Nf3 d5 2.g3 c6 3.Bg2 Bg4 4.0-0 e6 5.d3 Bxf3!? (The same dark-squared strategy we saw in the previous game. But it seems more accurate to defer this exchange until [after White's e2-e4) the pawn trade ...dxe4, dxe4. See White's 10th move) **6.Bxf3 Nf6 7.Nd2 Nbd7 8.e4 Bc5 9.Qe2 dxe4 10.dxe4**

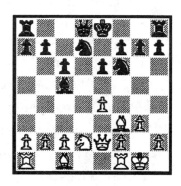

(More promising is 10.Nxe4!, keeping the h1-a8 diagonal open and retaining a slight pull. This would exploit Black's premature 5...Bxf3) **10...Qc7** (White threatened to gain space by 11.e5, so this or 10...e5 is indicated. The advantage of not playing ...e5 is that Black has e5 available for his pieces – at least for the time being) **11.Nc4** (11.a4 seems more accurate) **11...b5 12.Ne3 0-0 13.Bd2 Nb6 14.Bg2 Rfd8 15.Ba5 Qe5 16.Bc3 Bd4** (Black has gained some counterplay on the dark-squares) **17.f4 Qc5 18.Bxd4 Rxd4 19.c3 Rd7 20.Kh1 Rad8 21.Rad1 h6 22.Rxd7 Rxd7 23.e5 Nfd5 24.Nxd5 cxd5 25.f5** (He must play actively, otherwise Black would take the initiative by a minority attack on the Queenside **25...Nc4** (On 25...exf5 26.e6! Re7 27.exf7+ Rxf7 28.Qe8+ Qf8 29.Qxb5 White is on top) **26.fxe6 fxe6 27.Bh3 Re7 28.b3 Qe3 29.Qxe3!** (White stands better in this ending) **29...Nxe3 30.Rf3 Nc2 31.Kg1 Ne1 32.Re3 Nc2 33.Rf3** (Stronger was 33.Re2 Na3 34.Kf2 Kf7

35.Ke3 Rc7 36.Kd4 a5 37.Rf2+ Ke7 38.Bf1 and Black will have to fight for the draw) **33...Ne1 34.Re3 Nc2 Draw.**

Game 59
Ubilava-Rodriguez
Linares Open 1994

1.Nf3 d5 2.g3 Nf6 3.Bg2 c6 4.0-0 Bg4 5.d3 Nbd7 6.Nbd2 e5 7.h3 Bh5 8.Nh4 Bc5 9.Qe1 (For 9.c3 see Game 48) 9...0-0 10.e4 Re8 11.Nb3 Bf8 12.Bg5 (Threatening to take on d5; but this is easily met and the QB is then doing nothing on g5. Better was 12.a4 or 12.Bd2) **12...Qc7 13.a4 a5 14.Kh1 b6 15.Nf5**

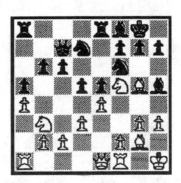

(Heading for e3 to pressure d5 [then ...dxe4, dxe4 leaves c4 for this Knight]. But Black finds a simple and good reply) **15...Bg6!** (Now 16.Ne3 drops the e-pawn) **16.Qe2 h6 17.Bd2 Bxf5!** (Displacing the e4-pawn and preparing to take the initiative in the center) **18.exf5 Rad8 19.Rg1** (Hoping for a later attack by g4-g5. But Black's centralized play is stronger) **19...c5 20.Be3 Bd6 21.g4 e4! 22.Bc1 d4!** (A fine pawn sacrifice to invade and blockade the dark-squares while opening up lines in the center) **23.dxe4 Bf4 24.Bxf4 Qxf4 25.Rae1 d3!!** (Another dynamic pawn thrust. Now if 26.Qxd3 then 26...c4! 27.Qxc4 Ne5 28.Qc3 Rd3!! 29.cxd3 Nexg4! 30.hxg4 Nxg4 and mate follows [a triumph on the dark-squares!]. Better is 29.Qxd3, but then 29...Nxd3 30.cxd3 Qxf2 favors Black) **26.cxd3 Ne5** (Threatening 27...Nxg4! as well as d3)

27.Qe3 Qxe3 28.Rxe3 Nxd3 29.Rf1 Nxb2 (The smoke has cleared, leaving Black with a big advantage) **30.e5 Nd5 31.Bxd5 Rxd5 32.e6 fxe6 33.fxe6 Rd6 34.e7 Nxa4 35.Rfe1 c4 36.Nc1 Nc5 37.f4 Kf7 38.Na2 Rd7 39.Nc3 Rdxe7 40.Rxe7+ Rxe7 White Resigns.**

Game 60
Karasev-Zarubin
St.Petersburg Open 1994

1.**Nf3 d5 2.g3 c6 3.Bg2 Bg4 4.h3 Bh5 5.0-0 Nd7 6.d3 e6 7.Nbd2 Bd6 8.b3 Ne7**

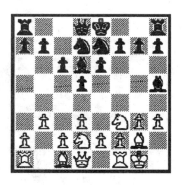

(This development of the KN introduces another variant of the Keres System. The main idea behind this deployment is to allow the f-pawn to play to either f5 or f6. In the former case, Black hopes to achieve a sort of "improved" Dutch Defense [Stonewall Variation] since the Black QB – which is usually hemmed-in behind the "wall" of pawns – is outside of the Stonewall pawn chain. In the latter case, f6 controls e5 and may form the prop for the formation of a full pawn center with e6-e5) **9.Bb2 f6 10.c4** (White will attack d5 by playing both c4 and e4) **10...0-0 11.e4** (By holding the option of opening the e-file, White hopes to make use of a drawback of 9...f6 – the weakening of the e6-square) **11...Re8 12.d4** (A delayed central advance; a hallmark of the hypermodern-style of play) **12...Bb4 13.Qc2 Bg6 14.a3 Bd6 15.Nh4 Bf7 16.f4!** (White rightly takes the opportunity to dominate the center with pawns) **16...dxe4 17.Nxe4**

Bc7 18.Rad1 Nf8 19.Rfe1 (White's opening strategy has been exemplary. All of his pieces are well-placed and Black's weakened e6 is exposed on the e-file) **19...Bb6 20.Kh2 Rc8 21.Nc5! Bxc5 22.dxc5** (The doubling of the c-pawns is meaningless, while the opening of the a1-h8 diagonal and the pressure on d6 increase White's advantage) **22...Qc7 23.b4 Rcd8 24.Re3 Rxd1 25.Qxd1 Rd8 26.Rd3 Rxd3 27.Qxd3** (Black has removed some of White's pressure by trading off the Rooks; but, White still holds all the trumps here: the two Bishops, more space, and the target on e6) **27...Qd7 28.Qd6 Nc8 29.Qd4 Qxd4 30.Bxd4 Nd7 31.Nf3 Ne7 32.g4!** (Gaining more space) **32...Ng6 33.Be3 e5 34.f5** (Now White has a strong square for his pieces on e4) **34...Ne7 35.Nd2 g6 36.Be4 Kf8 37.Kg3 Ke8 38.Kf2 gxf5 39.gxf5 Kd8 40.Ke2 Bh5+ 41.Kd3 Kc7 42.Nf1 Bf7 43.Bf2 Be8 44.Ne3 a5 45.Ng4 axb4 46.axb4 Bf7 47.Bg3** (Threatening 48.Nxf6 Nxf6 49.Bxe5+) **47...Kd8 48.Kc3 Ke8 49.Bh4 Ng8 50.Bd3 Ke7 51.Bf2 Kf8 52.b5 Ne7 53.Kb4 Kg7 54.Be4 Be8 55.Be3 Bf7 56.Bh6+ Kg8 57.Ne3 Kh8 58.Nc2 Bh5 59.Ne1 Be2 60.Nc2 Bf1 61.h4 Kg8 62.Bd2 Kf7 63.Ne3 Be2 64.Bc1 Ke8 65.Ba3 Kd8 66.Ka4 Kc7 67.Bb4 Kc8 68.Ka5 Kc7 69.Ba3 Kc8 70.Kb4 Kb8 71.Bc1 Kc7 72.Bd2 Kd8 73.Be1 Kc7 74.Bf2 Nc8 75.Bc2 Bf3 76.Nf1 Ne7 77.Ng3 Kd8 78.Kc3 Kc7 79.Be3 cxb5 80.cxb5 Nd5+ 81.Kd2 Nxe3 82.Kxe3 Bg2 83.b6+ Kc8 84.Ne4 Kb8 85.Ba4 Nf8 86.Nd6 Bh3 87.Kf3 Bf1 88.Ke3 Bh3 89.c6 bxc6 90.Bxc6 Bf1 91.Ne8 Bh3 92.Nc7 Bf1 93.Nd5 Bg2 94.h5 h6 95.Ne7 Bxc6 96.Nxc6+ Kb7 97.Ne7 Kxb6 98.Ng8 Black Resigns.**

Game 61
Stein-Ney
Parnu 1971

1.Nf3 d5 2.g3 c6 3.Bg2 Bg4 4.d3 Nd7 5.Nbd2 e6 6.0-0 Bd6 7.c4!? (Opting for an English-Reti; though varying from the "trademark" early e2-e4 of the KIA, often White – as in this game – will complement this early c4 with a later e2-e4. This is effectively the same procedure as if

White had played the usual e2-e4 first, and only later c2-c4) **7...Ngf6 8.b3 a5 9.Bb2 a4?!** (Aiming to cramp White. Then he would have an isolated White a-pawn to pressure down the a-file. However, as Stein demonstrates, the time it takes Black to win back the pawn allows White to seize the initiative in the center)

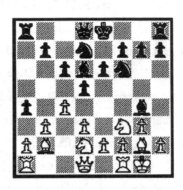

10.bxa4! Qa5 11.cxd5 cxd5 12.e4 0-0 (Of course not 12...Qxa4?? 13.Qxa4 Rxa4 14.e5) **13.h3 Bxf3** (Not 13...Bh5?? 14.g4 and 15.e5. Hence White gains the two Bishops by force) **14.Nxf3 dxe4 15.dxe4 Be7** (On 15...Nxe4? White has 16.Re1 and if 16...f5 then 17.Ng5!, while 16...Ndc5 is met by 17.Qd4! e5 18.Nxe5 and the long diagonal has a destructive effect on Black's position. Note how the opening of lines in the center works in perfect harmony with the two Bishops) **16.Qe2 Qxa4 17.Rfd1 Nc5 18.e5** (True, this blocks the QB's diagonal, but the cramping effect of the e5-pawn combined with the clearance of the KB's diagonal maintain strong pressure) **18...Nd5 19.Nd4 Nb6** (White threatened to play 20.Nf5!, taking advantage of the "overworked" e6-pawn. Notice that this shows the immediate effect of the newly opened h1-a8 diagonal) **20.Nb5!** (Threatening to invade d6, or double up on the d-file by 21.Rd4) **20...Qc4** (Trying to reduce the pressure by going into an ending. But two Bishops in this open position give White much the better chances) **21.Qxc4 Nxc4 22.Bd4 Ra5 23.Rdc1!** (Typical of Stein's mercurial style; instead of defending he counterattacks) **23...Rxb5**

24.Rxc4 Nd3? (Preferable was 24...b6, though even so 25.a4 Ra5 26.Bc3 Ra6 27.Bc6 Black is still tied up by the raking effect of White's Bishops, not to mention the fact that the b6-pawn is vulnerable) **25.a4 Nxe5 26.Rc7 Bd6 27.axb5** (Also good is simply 27.Rxb7) **27...Bxc7 28.Bc5 Rd8 29.b6 Bb8 30.Ra8 f6 31.Bxb7 Kf7 32.Kg2 Nd7 33.Be3 Ke7 34.Bf3 h6 35.b7 Bd6 36.Rc8 Nb8 37.Bb6 Rf8 38.Bc7 Bxc7 39.Rxc7+ Kd6 40.Rxg7 Rh8 41.Rg4 Nd7 42.Rd4+ Kc7 43.Rc4+ Kb8 44.Ra4 Kc7 45.Ra6 Re8 46.Ra3 Nb8 47.g4 Re7 48.Rc3+ Kb6 49.Rc8** (Now after 49...Ka7 50.Rh8 picks up the h-pawn) **Black Resigns.**

Game 62
Panno-Korchnoi
Palma de Mallorca 1972

1.Nf3 Nf6 2.g3 d5 3.Bg2 c6 4.0-0 Bg4 5.d3 Nbd7 6.Nbd2 e5 7.h3 Bh5 8.e4 dxe4 9.dxe4 Qc7 10.Qe1 (Nowadays this is a routine unpinning operation) **10...Nc5?!** (This allows White to gain some Queenside space "free of charge". Better was 10...Be7 or 10...Bxf3) **11.Nc4 Nfd7 12.b4!**

12...Ne6 13.a4 f6 14.c3 (After White's pawns have been allowed to expand on the Queenside, he will now center his pressure there) **14...Nb6 15.Nfd2 Qf7 16.Na5!** (Pressuring Black's Queenside, while discouraging the natural 16...Be7) **16...Bd6 17.Ndb3 Qc7 18.Be3 0-0 19.Qb1!** (Angling for 20.Nc5 and if 20...Bxc5 21.bxc5 Nd7 22.Qxb7) **19...Qe7**

20.Nd2 (White regroups his minor pieces and looks toward advancing his a-pawn [see move 25], to further strain the Black defenses on the Queenside) **20...Rad8 21.Nab3 Nc8 22.Re1 Rd7 23.Nc4 Rfd8 24.Qc2** (Both sides continue to maneuver, but it is White who has the superior coordination between his pieces and pawns) **24...Bc7 25.a5!** (Fixing Black's Queenside pawns and preparing to exploit their immobility by Nc5) **25...Qf7 26.Bf1 Kh8 27.Nc5!** (Forcing the following favorable exchange which will expose the Queenside pawns to direct pressure on the newly opened lines) **27...Nxc5 28.bxc5 Ne7 29.a6!** (Now all of Black's Queenside pawns will be isolated targets for White's forces) **29...bxa6 30.Rxa6 Bb8 31.Raa1** (Note that Black's Bb8 is locked out of play; this, plus his weak pawns cause Korchnoi to try a desperate pawn thrust striving for counterattack before White's obvious positional advantage is turned to account) **31...f5?! 32.exf5 Nxf5 33.Bg5!** (Winning material) **33...Re8 34.g4 h6 35.Bd2 Nh4 36.gxh5 Nf3+ 37.Kh1 e4 38.Bg2 Rxd2 39.Nxd2 Qf4** (At first glance it may seem that Black has stirred up a dangerous counterattack, but Panno's simple reply quickly refutes any such notion) **40.Nf1 Nxe1 41.Rxe1 Qf5 42.Rxe4 Rf8 Black Resigns.**

Game 63
Gorbatow-Mukhametov
Orel 1994

1.Nf3 d5 2.g3 Bg4 3.Bg2 Nd7 4.0-0 c6 5.d3 e6 6.Nbd2 Bd6 7.b3 Ne7 8.Bb2 0-0 9.Qe1 c5 10.e4 Nc6 11.Rc1 Qc7 12.Nh4 Rae8 13.f4 dxe4 14.dxe4?! (The right way to retain a pull was 14.Nxe4!) **14...f6 15.Nc4 Nd4 16.Nf3 e5 17.f5 Bh5 18.Ne3 b5 19.g4 Bf7 20.Nd2 c4 21.c3**

(see next diagram)

21...Nc5 22.cxd4 Nd3 23.Qe2 Nxb2 24.d5 Nd3 25.Ra1 Nf4 26.Qf3 Bb4 27.Rfd1 cxb3 28.Nxb3 Ba3 29.Bf1 Qb6 30.Kh1 Rc8 31.Ng2 Nxg2 32.Qxg2 a5 33.Qg1 Qa6 34.Bd3 Rc3 35.Qf1 Rb8 36.Rab1 Qb6

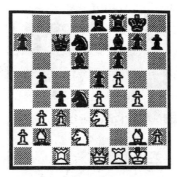

After 21.c3

37.Qg1 Qd8 38.Qf1 Be8 39.Na1 Rc5 40.Nc2 b4 41.Nxa3 bxa3
42.Rxb8 Qxb8 43.Rb1 Qc7 44.Qd1 Rc3 45.Kg2 h6 46.Rb3 Rc1
47.Qd2 Kh7 48.Qf2 a4 49.Rb1 Rc3 50.Rd1 Bd7 51.Rd2 Qd6 52.Qe2
Rc1 53.Rd1 Rc3 54.Rd2 Rc1 **Draw.**

Game 64
Mrva-Lechtynsky
Czechoslovakia Teams 1994

1.g3 d5 2.Bg2 c6 3.Nf3 Bg4 4.b3 Nd7 5.Bb2 Ngf6 6.h3?! Bxf3!
7.Bxf3 e6 8.d3 Bd6 9.e4!? (After 9.Nd2!? 0-0 10.0-0 h5! Black has the
initiative) 9...0-0 10.0-0 Qe7 11.Bg2 Rfd8 12.Qe2 dxe4 13.dxe4 e5!
14.f4? (Best was 14.Nd2!? Nf8 15.Nc4 Bc7 16.f4 exf4 17.gxf4 Ng6
18.e5 Nd5 with unclear play and mutual chances) 14...exf4 15.gxf4 Nd5
16.Qd2 Bc5+ 17.Bd4 N5f6 18.Re1 Nh5 19.c3 Nf8 20.f5 Qe5! 21.Rd1
Ng3 22.Qe3

(see next diagram)

22...Nxf5 23.Qg5 Nxd4 **White Resigns.**

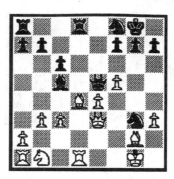

After 22. Qe3

Game 65
Stratil-Netusil
Czechoslovakia Teams 1994

1.g3 d5 2.Bg2 Nf6 3.Nf3 Bg4 4.d3 Nbd7 5.h3 Bxf3 6.exf3 e5 7.0-0
Bd6 8.Nc3 c6 9.Ne2 0-0 10.d4 Re8 11.dxe5 Nxe5 12.Nd4 Ng6 13.c3
a5 14.h4 h6 15.Nf5 Bc5 16.Qd2 Nh5 17.f4

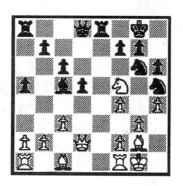

17...Nxg3 18.Nxg3 Qxh4 19.Qd3 Nxf4 20.Bxf4 Qxf4 21.Qf3 Qg5
22.Rae1 g6 23.Rd1 Re6 24.Rd3 Rae8 25.Qd1 Rf6 26.Qd2 Qh4 27.a3
Re5 28.b4 axb4 29.axb4 Bb6 30.Rd4 Bxd4 31.cxd4 Rg5 32.Re1 Rg4
33.Re8+ Kg7 34.Qe3 Rxd4 35.Qe7 Rd1+ 36.Bf1 Qxg3+ 37.fxg3
Rdxf1+ 38.Kg2 R6f2+ 39.Kh3 Rh1+ 40.Kg4 h5+ White Resigns.

Game 66
Smejkal-Chernin
New York 1988

1.Nf3 d5 2.g3 c6 3.Bg2 Bg4 4.0-0 Nd7 5.d3 e6 6.e4 Bd6 7.Nbd2 Ne7 8.h3 Bh5 9.d4 0-0 10.c3 Bc7 11.Re1 Re8 12.Qb3 Bb6 13.Nf1 dxe4 14.Rxe4

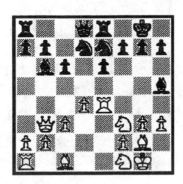

14...c5 15.Bg5 Bxf3 16.Bxf3 cxd4 17.cxd4 h6 18.Bd2 Nc6 19.Bc3 e5 20.Rae1 Nxd4 21.Qd1 Qc7 22.Bg2 Nb5 23.Ne3 Nxc3 24.bxc3 Bxe3 25.R4xe3 Rad8 26.Qe2 Rf8 27.Rd3 Rde8 28.Rd5 b6 29.Qe3 e4 30.a4 Nc5 31.a5 Nd3 32.axb6 axb6 33.Rb1 Re6 34.Rdb5 Nc5 35.c4 Rd8 36.Bf1 Rdd6 37.R5b2 Qe7 38.Ra2 Qg5 39.Qxg5 hxg5 40.Re1 f5 41.Ra8+ Kf7 42.Ra2 Kf6 43.Rb2 f4 44.Kh2 Kf5 45.Kg1 f3 46.Reb1 g4 White Resigns.

Game 67
Timman-Yusupov
Linares 1992

1.Nf3 d5 2.g3 c6 3.Bg2 Bg4 4.b3 Nd7 5.Bb2 Ngf6 6.d3 e6 7.0-0 Bd6 8.c4 0-0 9.Na3 Re8 10.Nc2 a5 11.Rc1 Bh5 12.Re1 Qb6 13.Rb1 Qa7 14.a3 Rad8 15.Qd2 e5 16.Nh4

16...Bc5 17.e3 dxc4 18.bxc4 Bf8 19.d4 Nc5 20.f3 exd4 21.exd4 Nb3 22.Qf4 b5 23.Bf1 Rxe1 24.Rxe1 Bd6 25.Qe3 a4 26.cxb5 cxb5 27.Bxb5 Qb8 28.Bxa4 Na5 29.Bc1 Nc4 30.Qe2 Rc8 31.Bg5 Nd5 32.Bd7 Rc7 33.Bf5 Bf8 34.Qe4 Nc3 35.Qd3 g6 36.g4 gxf5 37.gxh5 Nd5 38.Qxf5 Nd6 39.Qxd5 Rxc2 40.Bf4 h6 41.Nf5 **Black Resigns.**

Game 68
Azmayparashvili-Vaganian
USSR 1983

1.g3 d5 2.Bg2 Nf6 3.d3 c6 4.Nf3 Bg4 5.Nbd2 Nbd7 6.0-0 e6 7.b3 Bd6 8.Bb2 0-0 9.Re1 Re8 10.e4 e5 11.h3 Bh5 12.exd5?! cxd5 13.g4 Bg6 14.Nh4 Nf8 15.Nf1 Qc7! 16.g5?! Nh5 17.Ne3 d4 18.Nd5 Qd8 19.Nxg6 hxg6 20.h4 Rc8 21.Rc1 Ne6 22.Qg4?

22...Qa5 23.c4 Qxa2 24.Qd1 Nhf4 25.Ra1 Qxb2 26.Rb1 Qa3 27.Ra1 Nxg2 28.Rxa3 Nxe1 29.Rxa7 Nxd3 30.Qxd3 e4 31.Qxe4 Nf4 32.Qb1 Nxd5 33.cxd5 Re2 34.Ra2 d3 35.Kf1 Rxa2 36.Qxa2 Bb4 37.d6 d2 **White Resigns.**

Game 69
Kindermann-Gelfand
Munich 1991

1.g3 d5 2.Nf3 Nf6 3.Bg2 c6 4.0-0 Bg4 5.d3 Nbd7 6.Nbd2 e5 7.h3 Bh5 8.e4 dxe4 9.dxe4 Bc5 10.Qe1 0-0 11.Nc4 Re8 12.a4 Qc7 13.Nh4 Bf8 14.Bg5 Bg6 15.Nxg6 hxg6 16.Qe2

16...Nc5 17.Bxf6 gxf6 18.h4 Bh6 19.b4 Ne6 20.c3 b5 21.axb5 cxb5 22.Ne3 Qxc3 23.Nd5 Qc4 24.Nxf6+ Kf8 25.Qxc4 bxc4 26.Nxe8 Kxe8 27.Rac1 Rc8 28.Bh3 Bxc1 29.Bxe6 fxe6 30.Rxc1 c3 31.Kg2 Kf7 32.Kf3 Rc4 33.Ke3 Kf6 34.Kd3 Rxb4 35.Rxc3 g5 36.h5 g4 37.Rc7 Rb3+ 38.Kd2 Rb2+ 39.Ke3 Rb3+ 40.Ke2 Rb4 41.h6 Rxe4+ 42.Kf1 Rb4 43.h7 Rb1+ 44.Ke2 Rh1 45.Rxa7 Kg6 46.Ke3 Kf5 47.Rg7 Kf6 48.Rxg4 Rxh7 49.Ke4 Ra7 50.Rg8 Ra4+ 51.Kf3 Kf7 52.Rb8 **Draw.**

Game 70
Ljubojevic-Van der Wiel
Amsterdam 1991

1.Nf3 d5 2.g3 c6 3.Bg2 Bg4 4.d3 Nd7 5.Nbd2 e6 6.0-0 Bd6 7.b3 Ne7 8.Bb2 0-0 9.h3 Bh5 10.e4 c5 11.Qe1 Nc6 12.Nh2 Nd4

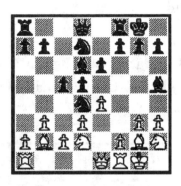

13.Bxd4 cxd4 14.exd5 exd5 15.Bxd5 Qc7 16.Nc4 Rae8 17.Qd2 Re2 18.Qg5 Bg6 19.Nf3 Be7 20.Qf4 Qxf4 21.gxf4 Rxc2 22.Nxd4 Rc3 23.Bxb7 Bf6 24.Nb5 Rxd3 25.Rad1 Nc5 26.Bg2 a6 27.Nc7 Rfd8 28.Nd5 Rxd1 29.Rxd1 Kf8 30.Bf3 Bh4 31.Ne5 Bf5 32.Kg2 Ne6 33.Nc4 Bc2 34.Rd2 Bb1 35.Kf1 g6 36.b4 h5 37.a3 Bf5 38.Kg2 g5 39.fxg5 Nxg5 40.Bxh5 Rxd5 41.Rxd5 Be4+ 42.f3 Bxd5 43.Ne3 Bc6 44.Nf5 Be1 45.Nd4 Bd7 46.Bg4 Ne6 47.Nxe6+ fxe6 48.f4 Bd2 49.Be2 Bb5 50.Kf3 Ke7 51.Bd1 Bd3 52.h4 Kf6 53.Kg4 e5 54.fxe5+ Kxe5 55.Kf3 Kd4 56.Be2 Kc3 57.a4 Kxb4 58.Bxd3 Kxa4 59.Bxa6 Draw.

Game 71
Miles-Dlugy
US Championship 1988

1.Nf3 d5 2.g3 Bg4 3.Bg2 c6 4.b3 e6 5.Bb2 Nf6 6.d3 Be7 7.0-0 0-0 8.Nbd2 Bh5 9.c4 c5 10.cxd5 Nxd5 11.Rc1 Nd7 12.Ne4 Bg6 13.a3 Rc8 14.Rc2 Qb6 15.Nfd2 Qa6 16.Qa1 f6 17.Rfc1 Rcd8 18.Nc3 Nc7 19.Qb1 Bf7 20.Ba1 e5 21.b4 b6 22.Nc4 Rfe8

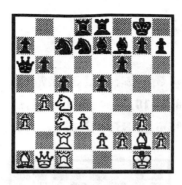

23.b5 Qc8 24.a4 Ne6 25.Ra2 Nd4 26.e3 Nf5 27.a5 Qb8 28.axb6 Nxb6 29.Na5 Bxa2 30.Qxa2+ Kh8 31.Nc6 Qc7 32.Nxd8 Rxd8 33.Qe6 Nd6 34.Bb2 c4 35.Ne4 Nxb5 36.dxc4 Na3 37.c5 Nbc4 38.Nd6 Bxd6 39.cxd6 Qxd6 40.Qxd6 Rxd6 41.Bxa3 Black Resigns.

Game 72
Neimann-Adams
France 1989

1.Nf3 Nf6 2.g3 d5 3.Bg2 c6 4.0-0 Bg4 5.d3 Nbd7 6.Nbd2 e5 7.h3 Bh5 8.Qe1 Bc5 9.e4 0-0 10.Nh4 Re8 11.Nb3 Bf8 12.g4?! Bg6 13.g5 Nh5 14.Nxg6 hxg6 15.exd5 cxd5 16.Bxd5

16...Nf4! 17.Bxf4 exf4 18.Qa5 Qxg5 19.Kh2 Re5 20.c4 Bd6 21.Rg1 Qh4 22.Rxg6 f3 23.Kg1 Rg5+ White Resigns.

Game 73
Ribli-Tal
Montpellier 1985

1.Nf3 d5 2.g3 Bg4 3.Bg2 c6 4.b3 Nd7 5.Bb2 Ngf6 6.0-0 e6 7.d3 Bc5 8.Nbd2 0-0 9.e4 dxe4 10.dxe4 e5 11.h3 Bxf3 12.Qxf3 Qe7 13.Rad1 b5 14.h4?! a5 15.c3 Nb6 16.Rfe1 Qe6! 17.Qf5

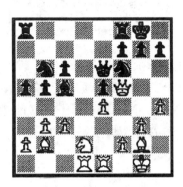

17...Ng4! 18.Re2 Rad8 19.Bf3 Rd3! 20.Kg2 Nxf2! 21.Rxf2 Bxf2 22.Kxf2 Qd6 23.Bc1 g6 24.Qg5 f6 25.Qh6 f5 26.Kg2 Rxf3! 27.Nxf3 Qxd1 28.Ng5 White Resigns.

Game 74
Azmayparashvili-Neverov
USSR 1986

1.g3 d5 2.Bg2 Nf6 3.d3 c6 4.Nd2 e5 5.e4 Bc5 6.Ngf3 dxe4 7.dxe4 Bg4 8.0-0 Nbd7 9.Nc4 0-0 10.h3 Bh5 11.Qd3 Qc7 12.Bg5 Rfe8 13.a4 h6 14.Bd2 Rad8 15.Qe2! (15.b4 Nb6! =) 15...b5

(see next diagram)

16.Ba5 Nb6 17.Ncd2 b4 18.c3 bxc3 19.Bxc3 Bd4 20.a5? (20.Rfc1!) Nbd5! 21.Bxd4 exd4 22.Rfc1 Qb8 23.Qc4 Bxf3 24.Bxf3 Nb4! 25.Qb3 Re5 26.Nc4 Rb5 27.e5 Nd7! 28.Nd6 Nxe5 29.Nxb5 Qxb5 30.Bg2 d3 31.Rc3 c5 32.Qd1! Rd4?! (32...g6) 33.Qh5! Nc2 34.Qxe5! Nxa1

After 15...b5

35.Rxc5 Qd7 36.Bd5 Nc2 37.Bb3 Nb4? 38.Rc7 Qd6 39.Bxf7+ Black Resigns.

Game 75
D. Byrne-Smyslov
Lugano 1968

1.g3 d5 2.Nf3 c6 3.Bg2 Bg4 4.0-0 Nd7 5.d3 e6 6.Nbd2 Bd6 7.e4 Ne7 8.Qe2 0-0 9.h3 Bh5 10.Re1 Kh8 11.d4 Rc8 12.c4

12...c5! 13.cxd5 exd5 14.e5 Bb8 15.e6 fxe6 16.Qxe6 Re8 17.dxc5 Nxc5 18.Qe2 Nc6 19.Qf1 Qf6 20.a4 Rxe1 21.Nxe1 Nd4 22.Bxd5 Ne2+ 23.Kh2 Qe5 24.Bg2 Nxg3 25.fxg3 Qxg3+ 26.Kg1 Qh2+ 27.Kf2 Bg3+ 28.Ke3 Bxe1 White Resigns.

Game 76
Kirov-Geller
Skara 1980

1.Nf3 d5 2.g3 c6 3.Bg2 Bg4 4.0-0 Nf6 5.d3 Nbd7 6.Nbd2 e6 7.h3
Bh5 8.Qe1 Be7 9.e4 0-0 10.Nh2?! (10.e5!? or 10.Nd4!?)

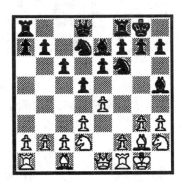

10...e5! 11.f4 exf4 12.gxf4 dxe4 13.dxe4 Nc5 14.Kh1 Re8 15.Nhf3 Bf8
16.Ne5 Nfd7! 17.Nxd7 Qxd7 18.Qh4 g6 19.a4 Rad8 20.Qf2 Qd4 21.e5
Qxf2 22.Rxf2 f5! 23.b3 Ne6 24.Nc4 Rd1+ 25.Rf1 Red8 26.Be3 Rxa1
27.Rxa1 Bh6 28.Nd6 Bxf4+ 29.Bxf4 Nxf4 30.Nxb7 Rd2 31.Bxc6 Rxc2
32.Nd8 Kf8! 33.Re1 Ke7 34.e6 Be2! White Resigns.

Game 77
Portisch-Ivkov
Amsterdam 1969

1.Nf3 d5 2.g3 c6 3.Bg2 Bg4 4.d3 e6 5.Nbd2 Bd6 6.0-0 Nd7 7.e4
Ne7 8.b3 0-0 9.h3 Bh5 10.Bb2 Rc8?! 11.Qe1 c5 12.Nh4 Qb6? 13.Qe3!
Rfe8

(see next diagram)

14.Qg5! Bg6 15.exd5 Nxd5 16.Nxg6 hxg6 17.Bxd5 exd5 18.Qxd5 Qc7
19.Nc4 Re6 20.Rae1 Rce8? 21.Nxd6 Black Resigns.

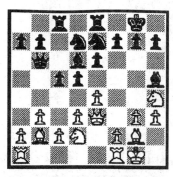

After 13...Rfe8

Game 78
Anic-Mitkov
Nice 1994

1.Nf3 d5 2.g3 Bg4 3.Bg2 Nd7 4.d3 e6 5.Nbd2 Bd6 6.h3 Bh5 7.0-0 Ne7 8.e4 c6 9.Qe1 Qb6 10.b3

10...Bxg3 11.exd5 cxd5 12.Nc4 dxc4 13.Be3 Qa6 14.fxg3 cxd3 15.c4 0-0 16.Qc3 Rac8 17.Bd4 Nf5 18.g4 Ng3 19.Rfe1 Bg6 20.Bxg7 Rfe8 21.Ne5 Rcd8 22.Bh6 Ne2+ 23.Rxe2 dxe2 24.Nxf7 Nf6 25.Nxd8 Rxd8 26.Bf3 Qb6+ 27.Kg2 e5 28.Qxe5 Re8 29.Bd5+ Kh8 30.Qc3 Be4+ 31.Bxe4 Rxe4 32.Re1 Qc6 33.Qf3 Kg8 34.Kf2 Nd7 35.Bf4 Nc5 36.Kg3 Ne6 37.Rxe2 Rxe2 38.Qxe2 Nd4 39.Qe3 Ne6 40.Qf3 Qb6 41.Qe3 Qa6 42.Bb8 Qc6 43.Be5 Qa6 44.Qh6 Qb6 45.c5 Qa6 46.Kh4 Qc6 47.Qf6

Qd5 48.Qh8+ Kf7 49.Qxh7+ Ke8 50.Bf6 Qxc5 51.Qg8+ Nf8 52.Bg7 Qe7+ 53.Kh5 Black Resigns.

Game 79
Nazarov-Nasybullin
USSR 1971

1.Nf3 d5 2.g3 c6 3.Bg2 Bg4 4.0-0 Nd7 5.d3 Ngf6 6.Nbd2 e5 7.h3 Bh5 8.e4 Bd6 9.Re1 0-0 10.c3 Re8 11.Qc2 Qc7 12.Nf1 Rad8 13.g4 Bg6 14.Ng3 Bf8 15.Bg5 h6 16.Bh4 Bh7 17.Nf5 g6

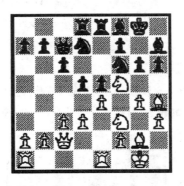

18.Nxh6+ Bxh6 19.g5 Bg7 20.gxf6 Bxf6 21.Bg3 dxe4 22.dxe4 Nc5 23.Nh2 Bg7 24.Bh4 Rd6 25.Rad1 f5 26.Rxd6 Qxd6 27.Rd1 Qe6 28.f3 Qxa2 29.Bf2 Bf8 30.Nf1 a5 31.Ne3 Kh8 32.Bf1 Qf7 33.Nc4 fxe4 34.Nd6 Bxd6 35.Rxd6 Ne6 36.Bc4 e3 37.Bg3 Qxf3 38.Bxe5+ Ng7 39.Rf6 e2 40.Qxe2 Qxe2 White Resigns.

Game 80
Portisch-Smyslov
Hastings 1970

1.Nf3 d5 2.g3 c6 3.Bg2 Bg4 4.d3 Nd7 5.0-0 e6 6.Nbd2 Bd6 7.h3 Bh5 8.Qe1 Ne7 9.b3 0-0 10.Bb2 a5 11.a4

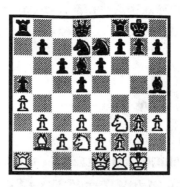

11...b5! 12.e4 bxa4 13.Rxa4 c5 14.Nh4 Nb6 15.Ra1 Nc6 16.f4 Be7 17.Nhf3 Bxf3! 18.Nxf3 a4 19.exd5 exd5 20.Ne5! Nxe5 21.fxe5 axb3 22.cxb3 Qd7 23.Rxa8 Nxa8 24.d4 Nc7 25.Qf2 Qb5 26.Qc2 Rb8 27.Qf2! Rf8 28.Qc2 Rb8 29.Qf2 Draw.

Game 81
Espig-Knaak
Leipzig 1977

1.Nf3 d5 2.g3 c6 3.Bg2 Bg4 4.b3 Nd7 5.Bb2 Qc7 6.0-0 e5 7.d3 Ngf6 8.Nbd2 Be7 9.h3 Bh5 10.e4 0-0 11.Re1

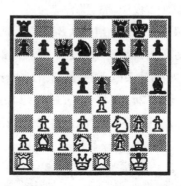

11...d4 12.g4 Bg6 13.Nh4 Rad8 14.Nf5 Bxf5 15.exf5 Bb4 16.a3 Bc3 17.Bxc3 dxc3 18.Nf1 Nd5 19.Bxd5 cxd5 20.d4 Rfe8 21.Re3 Qb6 22.Rxc3 exd4 23.Rd3 Ne5 24.Rg3 Rc8 25.Kg2 h6 26.Qd2 Nd7 27.Rd1 Re4 28.Rd3 Nf6 29.Ng3 Qd6 30.Nxe4 Nxe4 31.Qc1 Nxf2 32.Kxf2

Qh2+ 33.Kf3 Rxc2 34.R1d2 Qxh3+ 35.Kf4 Qxd3 36.Rxc2 Qe4+ 37.Kg3 d3 38.Rf2 d4 39.Qd1 Qe3+ 40.Rf3 Qe5+ 41.Kh3 Black Resigns.

Game 82
Azmaiparashvili-Yusupov
Las Palmas 1993

1.g3 d5 2.Bg2 c6 3.d3 Nf6 4.Nd2 e5 5.e4 Bd6 6.Ngf3 0-0 7.0-0 Bg4 8.h3 Bh5 9.Re1 Nbd7 10.exd5!? cxd5 11.g4 Bg6 12.Nh4 Nc5 13.Nb3 (13.Nf1!?) **13...Ne6 14.Nxg6 hxg6 15.c4 dxc4 16.dxc4 Rc8** (16...Qc7!? 17.Be3 Rad8 with the idea of b6) **17.Bxb7 Rxc4**

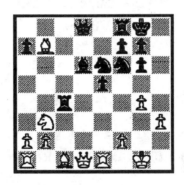

18.Ba6! (=) **18...Ra4 19.Bf1 Nf4 20.Be3 N6d5 21.Nd2 Rb4 22.a3 Nxe3?!** (Correct was 22...Rxb2! 23.Nc4 Nxe3 24.fxe3 Qh4 25.Nxb2 Qg3+ 26.Kh1 Nxh3 27.Bxh3 Qxh3+ 28.Kg1 Qg3+ 29.Kf1 Qh3+ with perpetual) **23.fxe3 Rxb2 24.Ne4! Nxh3+?** (24...Bc7! 25.Qxd8 Rxd8 26.exf4 Bb6+ 27.Kh1 f5 28.Ng5 Rdd2) **25.Bxh3 Qh4 26.Qf3! f5? 27.gxf5 gxf5 28.Nxd6 e4 29.Nxe4 fxe4 30.Be6+ Kh7 31.Qh3 Qxh3 32.Bxh3 Rf3 33.Bf1 Rg3+ 34.Kh1 Rb3 35.Bg2 Kh6 36.Bxe4 Rgxe3 37.Rxe3 Rxe3 38.Bc6 Rc3 39.Bb5 Kg5 40.a4 Rc7 41.Rd1! Rc8 42.Rd7 Ra8 43.Rxg7+ Kf5 44.Bc6 Rh8+ 45.Kg2 Rh6 46.Bb5 a6 47.Bd3+ Black Resigns.**

Game 83
Vaganian-Smagin
BRD 1991

1.Nf3 d5 2.g3 c6 3.Bg2 Bg4 4.b3 Nd7 5.Bb2 Ngf6 6.0-0 e6 7.d3 Bd6 8.Nbd2 0-0 9.e4 Qe7!? 10.a3 dxe4 11.dxe4 Be5 12.c3! Rfd8 13.Qc2 Bc7 14.a4 Bh5! 15.Rfe1 Bg6 16.Nc4

16...b5!? 17.Ba3 Qe8 18.Nb2! (18.Nd6? Bxd6 19.Bxd6 Nxe4!) 18...Bb6 19.c4 Nxe4!? 20.Rxe4 Nf6 21.Ne5 Bxe4 22.Bxe4 Bxf2+! 23.Kh1 (23.Kxf2? Rd2+!) 23...Nxe4 24.Qxe4 Rac8 25.Rf1 f5 26.Qf3 Bd4 27.Nbd3!? bxa4 28.b4 (28.bxa4? c5 =+) 28...Rc7! 29.Re1 a5 30.bxa5 Bc3 31.Rb1 Bxa5 32.Nc5 Ra8 33.Rd1 Bb6 34.Ncd7 Ba7! 35.Qd3 (35.Nxc6 Rxd7 36.Rxd7 Qxd7 37.Ne7+ Kf7 38.Qxa8 Qd1+ draws) 35...Rcc8 36.Bb2 (Agreed drawn, though it's still unclear)

Game 84
Salov-Bareev
Tilburg 1994

1.Nf3 d5 2.b3 Bg4 3.Bb2 Nd7 4.e3 c6 5.h3 Bh5 6.d3 e6 7.Nbd2 h6 8.g3 Ngf6 9.Bg2 a5 10.a3 Bd6 11.0-0 0-0 12.Qe1 Qb6 13.e4

(see next diagram)

13...Bxf3! (13...Bxg3?? 14.Bd4 c5 15.Bxf6; also, 13...e5 is met by 14.Nh4 focusing on f5) 14.Nxf3 e5 15.Nd2 Rfe8 16.Rb1 Rad8 17.Qe2

King's Indian Attack

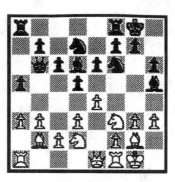

After 13.e4

Qc7 18.Rbe1 b5 19.Kh2 d4 20.Ra1! Rb8 21.h4 (21.Rfc1 h5!) 21...Nb6
22.Rfc1 c5 23.c3 Qd8 24.cxd4?! (Correct was 24.a4! bxa4 25.bxa4
Nxa4 26.Nc4 Nxb2 27.Nxb2 dxc3 28.Nc4! with an edge-Salov)
24...exd4! 25.f4!? (25.a4 bxa4 26.bxa4 Nxa4 27.Nc4 Nxb2 28.Nxb2
Nd5!; 25.b4 Na4 26.bxc5 Bxc5 unclear-Salov) 25...Nfd5 26.Qf3! Nxf4!
27.gxf4 Qxh4+ 28.Kg1 Bxf4 29.Rxc5! Be3+ 30.Kf1 Bxd2 31.Bxd4
Nd7 32.Rd5 Nf8 (32...Qe7 unclear. Salov) 33.Ke2! Qf4 34.Rf1 Ne6!?
35.Be5 Qxf3+ 36.Bxf3 Bg5 37.Bxb8 Rxb8 38.Kf2 Be7 39.a4 bxa4
40.bxa4 Rb2+ 41.Kg3 Bb4 42.Bg4 Ng5 43.Bd7 Kh7? (43...Re2 44.Bb5
Be1+ 45.Rxe1 Rxe1 46.Bc4 =) 44.Rxg5! hxg5 45.Rxf7 Be1+ 46.Kh3
Re2 47.Kg4 Re3? 48.Rf3! Re2 49.Kxg5 Bd2+ 50.Kf5 g6+ 51.Ke6 Bc3
52.Kd5! Kg7 53.d4 Bb2 54.Bb5 Rg2 55.e5 g5 56.e6 Rd2 57.e7 **Black
Resigns.**

Game 85
Vaganian-Adams
Ter Apel 1992

1.Nf3 Nf6 2.g3 d5 3.Bg2 c6 4.0-0 Bg4 5.d3 Nbd7 6.Nbd2 e5 7.e4
dxe4 8.dxe4 Bc5 9.a4!? 0-0?! (Better 9...a5, to stop a4-a5) 10.h3 Bh5
11.a5! Qc7 12.Qe2 b5 13.Nb3 Be7 14.g4! Bg6 15.Nh4 Nc5 (15...Bxe4?
16.Bxe4 Nxe4 17.Qxe4 Bxh4 18.g5) 16.Nf5 Ne6 17.Be3 Rab8

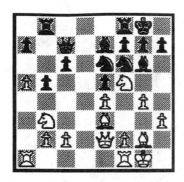

18.c4! Rfe8 (18...bxc4 19.Qxc4 Rb4 20.Qxc6! Bxf5 21.exf5 Qxc6 22.Bxc6 Nd8 23.Ba4 strongly favors White; but better was 18...Rfd8) **19.Rfc1 b4 20.c5 Bf8 21.Qc4 Red8 22.Rd1 h5 23.g5 Nd5** (23...Nd7 24.Nh4 Bh7 25.g6 wins) **24.exd5 cxd5 25.Rxd5 Rxd5?** (Relatively better was 25...Bxf5 though even so after 26.Rxd8 Nxd8 27.c6 Be6 28.Qc2 Rc8 29.Nc5! White is in control) **26.Nh4!! Rxc5** (26...Rd6 27.Nxg6 fxg6 28.Rc1 Rc8 29.cxd6 Qxc4 30.Rxc4 Rxc4 31.Bd5 winning) **27.Nxc5 Bxc5 28.Nxg6 Qd6** (28...Bxe3 29.Qxc7 Nxc7 30.Ne7+ Kf8 31.Nc6 ʼins) **29.Bxc5 Nxc5 30.Qd5! Qxd5 31.Bxd5 Rd8 32.Rd1 Black Resigns.**

Game 86
Ljubojevic-Illescas
Cordoba Linares 1993

1.Nf3 d5 2.g3 c6 3.Bg2 Bg4 4.d3 e6 5.Nbd2 Nd7 6.0-0 Bd6 7.e4 Ne7 8.h3 Bh5 9.Re1 0-0?! (9...Ne5!?) 10.g4! Bg6

(see next diagram)

11.e5 Bc7 12.Nf1 c5 13.Bg5 Qe8 14.Bh4 Nc6 15.Bg3 Qb8 16.Qe2 a5?! (16...Kh8 17.h4 f6! – unclear) **17.h4 f6 18.exf6 Nxf6 19.h5?** (19.Ng5!) **19...Bf7 20.Ng5 Bxg3 21.fxg3** (21.Nxg3 Nd4 22.Qd1 Qf4 strongly favors Black) **21...h6 22.Nxf7 Rxf7 23.c3 Re7 24.g5 hxg5 25.Qe3 Qd6** (25...Nxh5 =+) **26.Qxg5 Rf8 27.Re2 Nh7! 28.Qh4 Rf5 29.Rae1 Nf6**

After 10...Bg6

30.g4 Rf4 31.Nh2 e5 32.Qg3?! (32.Qh3! with the idea of g5 is unclear)
32...Rf7! 33.Rxe5!? Nxe5 34.Qxf4 Nfxg4 35.Qg5 Re7! 36.Nf1? (36.d4!
+=) **36...d4! 37.c4 Qf6! 38.Qd2 Qh4 39.Bd5+ Kh8 40.Re2 Rf7?**
(40...b6 -+) **41.Qxa5 Rf8 42.Qe1 Qf6 43.Be4 Qf4 44.b3 b6 45.Rg2 Rf5!**
46.Rg3 Rxh5 47.Qd2 g5?! (47...Ne3!) **48.Qxf4 gxf4 49.Rg2 Nf6**
50.Nd2 Rh3 51.Rxh2 Rxh2 52.Kxh2 Nxe4 53.dxe4 Kg7 54.Kg2 Kf6
55.a3 Nd3 56.Kf3 Ke5 57.Ke2 Nb2 58.Kf3 d3 59.Kg4? (59.b4!)
59...Nd1? (59...Kd4 -+) **60.b4! Nb2 61.bxc5 bxc5 62.Kf3 Na4 63.Nb3**
Nc3 64.Nd2 Na4 65.Nb3 Nb2 66.Nd2 Kd4 67.Kxf4 Kc3 68.Nf3 Nxc4
69.e5 d2 70.Nxd2 Kxd2 71.e6 Kd3 72.e7 Nd6 73.Ke5 Ne8 74.a4 c4
75.a5 c3 76.a6 c2 77.a7 c1=Q 78.a8=Q Qg5+ 79.Ke6 Qg8+ 80.Ke5
Qg5+ 81.Ke6 Nc7+ 82.Kd7 Nxa8 83.e8=Q Nb6+ (=+) **84.Kc6 Nc4**
85.Qd7+ Kc3 86.Qe6 Qg2+ 87.Kc7 Qg3+ 88.Kc6 Qf3+ 89.Kc7 Qf4+
90.Kc6 Qf2 91.Kb7 Qd4 92.Qe1+ Kb3 93.Qe6 Qc5 94.Ka6 Ka3
95.Qf6 Qa5+ 96.Kb7 Qd5+ 97.Kc7 Kb4 98.Qf8+ Ka5 99.Qe7 Ka6
100.Qf6+ Kb5 101.Qg6 Qe5+ 102.Kd8 Kc5 103.Qg1+ Kc6 104.Qg6+
Nd6 105.Qc2+ Kd5 106.Qd3+ Kc5 107.Qa3+ Kb6 108.Qb3+ Ka7
109.Qa2+ Kb7 110.Qb1+ Nb5 111.Qh1+ Kb6 112.Qh6+ Nd6
113.Qe6! Qxe6 Stalemate.

Game 87
Akopian-Beliavsky
Linares 1995

1.Nf3 d5 2.g3 Nf6 3.Bg2 c6 4.0-0 Bg4 5.b3 Nbd7 6.Bb2 e6 7.d3
Bd6 8.Nbd2 0-0 9.h3 Bh5 10.e4 dxe4

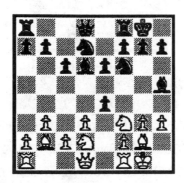

11.dxe4 Be5 12.c3 Bc7 13.Ba3 Re8 14.Qc2 a5 15.Nd4 Qb8 16.Rae1
a4 17.b4 Bg6 18.c4 Qa7 19.c5 Rad8 20.b5 Be5 21.b6 Qa6 22.N4f3
Bb8 23.Rb1 Ne5 24.Nxe5 Bxe5 25.Nc4 Bd4 26.Nd6 Rxd6 27.cxd6 e5
28.Rfd1 Nd7 29.Rb4 c5 30.Rxa4 Qxb6 31.Rb1 Qc6 32.Ra7 b5 33.Kh2
h5 34.f3 h4 35.Bf1 hxg3+ 36.Kg2 Rb8 37.Rxb5 Rxb5 38.Qa4 c4
39.Ra5 Bxe4 40.Qxb5 Bxf3+ 41.Kxg3 Qe4 White Resigns.

Game 88
Abramovic-Drasko
Yugoslavian Championship 1994

1.Nf3 d5 2.g3 c6 3.Bg2 Bg4 4.d3 Nd7 5.Nbd2 e6 6.e3 Bd6 7.Qe2
Ne7 8.h3 Bh5 9.g4 Bg6 10.Nh4

(see next diagram)

10...Qa5!? **11.c3** (11.0-0 h5 12.g5 Qa4! 13.Ndf3 e5 14.b3 Qa6 with the
idea of e5-e4 is equal) **11...Qa6 12.Nxg6 hxg6** (12...Nxg6 13.h4 Nge5
14.d4 Nd3+ 15.Kf1 +=) **13.Nb3?!** (Better 13.d4) **13...e5 14.f4?! f5!**
15.Bd2 0-0-0 16.Bf1 Rde8 17.Qg2 exf4 18.exf4 Qa4 19.d4 fxg4?!

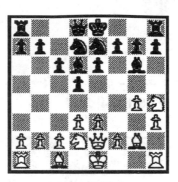

After 10.Nh4

(19...c5!) **20.0-0-0! c5** (20...Qxa2? 21.Kc2 Ba3 22.Rb1 threatening 23.Nc1) **21.Nxc5 Nxc5 22.dxc5 Bxc5 23.Qxg4+ Kb8 24.Bd3** (24.a3!?) **24...Qxa2 25.Bb1** (Better 25.Bxg6) **25...Qa1 26.Rhe1 Rc8 27.Qd7 Rhd8 28.Qb5 Nf5 29.Qb3 d4 30.Qa2 Qxa2 31.Bxa2 dxc3 32.bxc3 Ba3+ 33.Kb1 Rc6 34.Bb3 Rcd6 35.Ka2 Bc5 36.Bc1 Rxd1 37.Bxd1 Rd3 38.Bb2 Rxh3 39.Re6 Rg3 40.Bb3 Kc7 41.Re8 b5 42.Bd5 Ne7 43.Be4 Re3 44.Bb1 a5 45.c4 bxc4 46.Be5+ Kd7 47.Ra8 Re2+ 48.Ka1 Nc6 49.Bxg7 Bd4+ 50.Bxd4 Nxd4 51.Bxg6 c3 52.Kb1 Rb2+ 53.Kc1 Nb3+ 54.Kd1 Rd2+ 55.Ke1 c2 White Resigns.**

Game 89
Nenasev-Wedberg
Manila 1992

1.Nf3 Nf6 2.g3 d5 3.Bg2 c6 4.0-0 Bg4 5.d3 Nbd7 6.Qe1 e5 7.e4 dxe4 8.dxe4 Bc5 9.Nbd2 0-0 10.Nc4!? Re8

(see next diagram)

11.b4!? Be6 12.Nb2! Bf8 13.Ng5 Bg4 14.f3 Bh5 15.Bd2 Nb6?! (15...c5 16.b5 a6 17.a4 Nb6 18.Be3 axb5 19.axb5 Rxa1 20.Qxa1 +=) **16.a4!! h6 17.Nh3 Qd4+ 18.Rf2 Qxb2 19.Bc3 Bxb4 20.Bxb4 Qd4 21.g4 Bg6 22.g5! Nh5** (22...hxg5 23.Rd1 Qb2 24.a5! Nbd7 [24...Nc4 25.Bf1] 25.Rb1 Qa2 26.c3 Qc4 27.Bf1 Qe6 28.Nxg5 wins. Better 20...Nc8, but

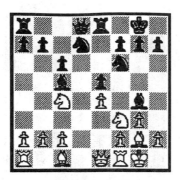

After 10....Re8

still winning for White. Nenasev) **23.Rd1 Qc4 24.Bf1 Qe6 25.Rd6 Qc8?**
(25...Qa2!, though White is still on top. Nenasev) **26.a5 Nd7 27.gxh6
Nf8** (27...gxh6 28.Qd2) **28.hxg7 Ne6 29.Bc3 Nef4 30.Nxf4 Nxf4
31.Rfd2 Kxg7 32.Qh4 Kg8 33.Qg5! Kh7 34.Kh1 b5 35.Bxe5 Nh5
36.Bd4 Rg8 37.Be3 Qf8 38.Bh3 Qg7 39.Rxg6! Qa1+** (39...Qxg6
40.Bf5, or 39...fxg6 40.Rd7! Qxd7 41.Qh6#) **40.Qg1 Black Resigns.**

Game 90
Kindermann-Gelfand
Munich 1991

1.g3 d5 2.Nf3 Nf6 3.Bg2 c6 4.0-0 Bg4 5.d3 Nbd7 6.Nbd2 e5 7.h3
Bh5 8.e4 dxe4 9.dxe4 Bc5 10.Qe1 0-0 11.Nc4 Re8 12.a4 Qc7 (12...a5!?)
13.Nh4! Bf8 14.Bg5! Bg6 15.Nxg6 hxg6 16.Qe2 Nc5 17.Bxf6 gxf6
18.h4 Bh6

(see next diagram)

19.b4! Ne6 20.c3 b5 21.axb5 cxb5 22.Ne3 Qxc3?! (Better 22...Bxe3 =)
**23.Nd5 Qc4 24.Nxf6+ Kf8 25.Qxc4 bxc4 26.Nxe8 Kxe8 27.Rac1!
Rc8!** (27...Bxc1?! 28.Rxc1 Rc8 29.Rc3! followed by Bf1) **28.Bh3 Bxc1
29.Bxe6 fxe6?!** (Better 29...Bd2! 30.Bxc8 c3) **30.Rxc1 c3 31.Kg2 Kf7
32.Kf3 Rc4 33.Ke3 Kf6 34.Kd3 Rxb4 35.Rxc3 g5! 36.h5 g4! 37.Rc7
Rb3+ 38.Kd2** (38.Kc4 Rb2 39.Rxa7 Kg5! draws) **38...Rb2+ 39.Ke3**

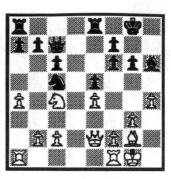

After 18...Bh6

**Rb3+ 40.Ke2 Rb4 41.h6 Rxe4+ 42.Kf1 Rb4 43.h7 Rb1+! 44.Ke2 Rh1
45.Rxa7 Kg6 46.Ke3 Kf5 47.Rg7 Kf6 48.Rxg4 Rxh7 49.Ke4 Ra7
50.Rg8 Ra4+ 51.Kf3 Kf7 52.Rb8 Draw.**

Game 91
**Hodgson-Van der Wiel
Wijk aan Zee 1993**

    **1.Nf3 Nf6 2.g3 d5 3.Bg2 c6 4.0-0 Bg4 5.d3 Nbd7 6.Nbd2 e6 7.h3
Bh5 8.e4** (On 8.c4 then 8...Bd6 with the idea of ...e6-e5) **8...Qc7 9.Qe2**
(9.Qe1!?) **9...dxe4 10.dxe4 Ne5!?** (To be considered was 10...e5!? and
if 11.g4 then 11...Bg6 12.Nh4 Nc5 13.Nf5 Ne6 with an edge for Black
due to the weakness of d4 and f4. After 10...e5!?, a better choice is 11.b3.
Another possibility is 10...h6) **11.Qe3** (11.g4 Nxf3+ 12.Nxf3 Bg6
13.Nh4 [13.Nh2 Bc5] 13...Be7! to answer 14.f4 with 14...Bxe4)
11...Nxf3+ (11...Nfd7 12.Nxe5 Qxe5 13.Nb3!) **12.Nxf3 Qb6?!** (Correct
was 12...Bxf3 =) **13.Ne5!**

(see next diagram)

    13...Qc5!? (13...Bc5 14.Qg5 [or 14.Qf4] 14...h6 15.Qxg7 Ke7
16.Qxf6+! Kxf6 17.Nd7+) **14.Qxc5 Bxc5 15.Re1?!** (15.Nd3! Bb6
16.Nf4 +=) **15...Nd7 16.Nd3** (16.Nc4 Nb6 =) **16...Bb6 17.a4 a5 18.Nf4
Bg6 19.h4 e5 20.Nxg6 fxg6! 21.Ra3?!** (21.Be3 =) **21...Rf8 22.Re2**

After 13.Ne5!

(22.Be3) **22...Nc5! 23.Ra1** (23.Be3 0-0-0) **23...Ne6 24.Be3 Bxe3 25.Rxe3 Rd8 26.Bf1! Nc5 27.Rc3! b6 28.Rc4 Rd2?** (28...Rd4!) **29.b4 axb4 30.a5! b3 31.axb6 Rxc2 32.Rxc5! b2! 33.Rxe5+?!** (33.Ra8+! Ke7 34.Rxf8 b1=Q 35.Rxc2 Kxf8 36.Rxc6 Ke7 37.Rc7+ Kd8 38.Rxg7 Qxb6 39.Rxh7) **33...Kd7?!** (33...Kf7!) **34.Rb1 Rfxf2 35.Bh3+! Kd6 36.Re8?** (36.Ra5!! +-) **36...Rf7 37.Rd8+ Kc5 38.Rdd1 Kxb6 39.Rf1?!** (39.Bf1!?) **39...Rxf1+ 40.Bxf1 Kc5 41.e5 Kd5 42.e6! Kxe6 43.Bd3 Rd2 44.Re1+ Kd5 45.Be4+ Kd4 46.h5! gxh5 47.Bxh7 c5 48.Re4+ Kc3 49.Re3+ Kc4 50.Re4+ Rd4?! 51.Re7?** (51.Re1!) **51...g6!! 52.Bxg6 Rd3 53.Bf7+ Kc3 54.Ba2 Rd1+ 55.Kf2 Ra1 White Resigns.**

CHAPTER THREE

The Karpov System

Game 92
Sznapik-Karpov
Skopje 1972

1.e4 c5 2.Nf3 e6 3.d3 (An important transpositional mode; White cleverly sidesteps the Sicilian labyrinth, forcing Black into the familiar channels of the KIA. This obviously has psychological value. The opponent is waiting with his hand practically hoovering over his c5-pawn, waiting to chop off your d-pawn after the expected 3.d4, when your hand – seemingly well on its way to d4 – instead suddenly stops at the KIA "drop-off" at d3) **3...Nc6 4.g3 d5 5.Nbd2 Bd6** (This and Black's following move introduce the Karpov System) **6.Bg2 Nge7**

(Completing the initial Karpov set-up. The main strategical idea behind this pattern is to control e5. As we saw in several early games in this book, when White can push e4-e5, attacking chances automatically follow. Karpov's System vies for control of e5 by placing the KN at e7 so that the f-pawn can be stationed at f6. This is a direct way of saying to White that e4-e5 will be difficult or impossible to enforce. Another option here for Black is the advance f7-f5 [normally played after White has pushed e2-e4], vying for control of e4 and reserving the aggressive option of ...f5-f4 with possibilities of attack against White's Kingside. Since in most variations of the KIA White tries to build up pressure against Black's Kingside, you can easily understand the "in your face" attitude of the Black player who opts for this latter course) **7.0-0 0-0 8.Re1 Bc7?!** (As we shall see this can be strongly answered by 9.exd5! – see Game 93) **9.c3 b6 10.e5** (Since in this game Karpov has eschewed an early f7-f6, White simply goes for the usual space-gainer e4-e5) **10...a5** (Compare this pawn pattern to the Kasparov-Sicilian System – the major difference being that Black has fianchettoed his KB in that pattern [and, as we saw, usually delayed castling Kingside]. Note that without the move ...g7-g6, Black's Kingside dark-squares are much better covered; hence he feels safer with early Kingside castling in this system) **11.Nf1 Ba6 12.h4** (Intending to "puncture" Black's Kingside pawn wall by h5-h6. This, of course, is intended to force a weakening of the initially well-protected Kingside dark-squares. If Black stops h5-h6 by playing ...h6 himself, then the Black h6-pawn can easily be a target for later sacrificial attacks – e.g., after Nf1-h2-g4 and then N or Bxh6) **12...d4** (Gaining more central space; but, as we will see, White has a chance to exploit this plan on move 15) **13.c4 Qd7** (After 13...Ng6 White plays 14.h5! Ngxe5 15.Nxe5 Nxe5 16.Bf4! Nd7 17.Bxa8 Bxf4 18.Bg2 and Black is simply down in material with no real compensation) **14.N1h2** (To be considered was 14.h5!?) **14...f5?!** (Better was 14...f6!? 15.exf6 gxf6 16.Bh3 Nf5 with complex play and chances for both players) **15.exf6?e.p.** (A serious error. Correct was 15.a4!. This would place Black in a slight strategical quandary, as his Queenside would be completely blocked, leaving White with almost a free hand to gradually increase the pressure against Black's Kingside. True, it would be difficult to breakthrough on the rather narrow front there [because Black's ...f7-f5 has provided some useful defensive space], but any winning chances would be on White's side. However, objectively speaking Black could very likely defend successfully) **15...gxf6 16.Ng4 e5!** (Now Black has a big advantage. His center closely resembles a bulldozer, which will slowly but surely smash White's strategically inert position) **17.Bh3 Qe8** (Avoiding the brash threat 18.Nh6+) **18.Bh6 Rf7 19.Bd2** (Threatening 20.Nh6+. But these tactical "pinpricks" cannot alter the strategical imbalance of the position) **19...Kh8 20.Kh2 Bc8 21.Qe2 Bd7 22.Ng1 f5** (The bulldozer shifts into a higher gear) **23.Nh6** (Forced; but this steed is rushed forward into the teeth of Black's machine) **23...Rg7 24.Bg5 Qg6 25.Bg2 Ng8! 26.Nxg8 Raxg8 27.Qd2 f4!** (Black has treated White's Knight, and now the forward Bishop, with cruel abandon; the danger is in a coming h7-h6) **28.Be4 Qd6 29.Qe2 Be8 30.Bd5 Rf8 31.gxf4 h6 32.fxe5 Qxe5+! 33.Qxe5 Nxe5 34.f4** (34.Bxh6 Ng4+ wins) **34...Ng4+ 35.Kg3 Ne3 White Resigns.**

Game 93
D'Amore-Valvo
New York 1990

1.Nf3 d5 2.g3 c5 3.d3 Nc6 4.Bg2 e6 5.0-0 Bd6 6.Nbd2 Nge7 7.e4 0-0 8.Re1 Bc7?! 9.exd5! (This is the way to cast doubt on 8...Bc7?!) **9...Nxd5** (To be considered was 9...exd5, though after 10.d4! cxd4 11.Nb3 Black will be saddled with an isolated d-pawn, this would only slightly favor White) **10.Ne4!** (Alert play. White sees the chance to open up the center to seize an early initiative) **10...b6 11.d4! cxd4** (11...c4?! 12.c3 leaves White with firm control of both d4 and e5, not to mention the vulnerability of Black's advanced c-pawn e.g., 12...Bb7 13.Qa4! Na5 14.Ne5 with the upper hand for White) **12.Nxd4 Bb7** (After 12...Nxd4 13.Qxd4 Bb7 14.c4 White is better) **13.Bg5 Nde7?**

(see next diagram)

(Failing to see the following surprise shot) **14.Nf6+!** (Now after 14...gxf6 15.Bxf6 [threatening 16.Qg4+] 15...Qe8 16.Nxc6 Bxc6 17.Qd2! [threatening 18.Qg5+ Ng6 19.Qh6] 17...Bxg2 18.Qg5+ mating in two. Or 14...Kh8 15.Qh5 h6 16.Bxh6! gxf6 17.Bg5+ Kg8 18.Bxf6 Ng6 19.Bxd8

After 13...Nde7?

Black suffers too much material loss. The personable and very talented master Michael Valvo is caught asleep at the switch, though his opponent deserves full credit for his aggressive tactics) **Black Resigns.**

Game 94
Calvo-Karpov
Madrid 1973

1.e4 c5 2.Nf3 e6 3.d3 Nc6 4.g3 d5 5.Nbd2 Bd6 6.Bg2 Nge7 7.0-0 0-0 8.Re1 Qc7 (An improvement on 8...Bc7?!, seen in the previous games) **9.b3?**

(This is a poor idea in this position. It has little real influence on the center and leaves permanent square weaknesses on the Queenside. The right way is 9.c3 – see the next game for this) **9...Bd7 10.Bb2 d4!**

(Promptly "stuffing" the White QB's scope on the long diagonal) **11.Nc4 e5** (Stopping the threat of 12.e5 while building a very strong central pawn wedge) **12.a4 b6 13.Qd2?!** (Better was 13.Nxd6 Qxd6 14.Nd2 with the idea of Rf1/Nc4/Bc1 and eventually f2-f4. After missing this chance, White soon falls into a listless position) **13...f6!** (Characteristically, Karpov proceeds with patient reinforcement of his position; there is no need to hurry. Also, the possibility of 14...g5 and a following ...Ng6 induces White to weaken his Kingside with the following move) **14.h4 Qb8!** (Intending to remove White's last chance for the trade Nxd6. But Calvo seems to not care) **15.Ba3?!** (15.Nxd6) **15...Bc7 16.Reb1?!** (He had to try for some activity by 16.b4!?) **16...Be6!** (Now 17.b4 is met by 17...Bxc4! 18.dxc4 cxb4 19.Bxb4 Nxb4 20.Qxb4 Bd6 and White's doubled, isolated c-pawns on the open c-file spell strategic doom) **17.Kh2 Qc8 18.Qe2 Bg4 19.Qf1 f5!** (With the idea of a further f5-f4. This type of attack is a sure indication of poor planning by White) **20.Ncd2** (After 20.exf5 Qxf5 the clearance of the e4-square is insufficient compensation for the tremendous pressure on the f-file) **20...f4 21.Bh3 h5!** (After 22.Bxg4? hxg4 White is squashed) **22.Qg2 Ng6 23.Ng5 Bd8 24.Ngf3 Be7 25.Rg1 Qe6 26.Raf1** (White's massed pieces on the Kingside are "all dressed-up with nowhere to go") **26...Rf7 27.Rh1 Raf8 28.Kg1 Qd6 29.Kh2 a6 30.Kg1** (White can only wait for the axe to fall) **30...Rf6 31.Bxg4?** (This only accelerates the end, but it is clear that White's position is hopeless) **31...hxg4 32.Ng5 f3** (Readers with sensitive temperaments should not look any further) **33.Qh2 Nh8 34.Rc1 Rh6!** (A tragi-comic tableau. White's Ng5 cannot be saved) **35.Nc4 Qc7 White Resigns.**

Game 95
Fischer-DiCamillo
New Jersey (Log Cabin Club Tourney) 1957

1.e4 e6 2.d3 d5 3.Nd2 Bd6 (A creative way to reach the Karpov line) **4.Ngf3 c5 5.g3 Nc6 6.Bg2 Nge7 7.0-0 0-0 8.Re1 Qc7 9.c3** (With ideas of playing for a later d3-d4 and/or b2-b4 [after a2-a3]. Of course the young Fischer could not have a complete awareness of all the fine points of this opening structure. But his gifted intuition anticipated the theoretical results – which are now known to specialists of the KIA) **9...Bd7 10.Qe2!** (Threatening 11.e5 and therefore provoking Black's response) **10...f6**

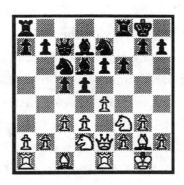

(As mentioned in our first game in this section, the move ...f7-f6 is a characteristic move in the Karpov System. Fischer's method of trying to exploit the slight weakening of e6 is very instructive) **11.a3 Rae8** (A natural developing move which shores up the potentially vulnerable e6-square. But this turns out to be inadequate in the long-run. Modern theory gives 11...Rac8 with ...b5 as a reasonable plan here for Black) **12.b4 b6 13.d4!** (The star move behind White's strategy. At first glance this move seems like a positional "lemon," leaving White with an isolated d-pawn. But a deeper look reveals that Black cannot exploit the purely optical weakness of the d-pawn because his possible vertical pressure against it on the d-file is blocked by the unfortunate placement of the Bishops on d6 and d7. As a result, the net effect of this advance is a gain of central influence, and [after Black's 14th move], the focussing of pressure against Black's backward e6-pawn by means of the newly opened e-file) **13...cxd4 14.cxd4 dxe4 15.Nxe4 Nd5 16.Bb2 Qb8 17.Nfd2!** (A fine maneuver to bring this Knight to a better post on c4) **17...Nd8** (To defend his e6 weakling, and trying to circulate his dormant

QB into play on the a8-h1 diagonal) **18.Nxd6 Qxd6 19.b5!** (Another astute move. Now his QB will find terrific activity along the a3-f8 diagonal after a3-a4) **19...Bc8 20.a4 Qd7 21.Ba3 Rf7 22.Nc4 Nb7 23.Qd3 Rd8 24.Be4!** (Provoking a further weakening of Black's pawns) **24...g5 25.Rac1 Ne7** (Now White will win material, though a good defensive plan is not be found anyway) **26.Bxb7! Bxb7 27.Nd6 Nf5** (After 27...Rff8 28.Nxb7 Qxb7 29.Rxe6 is winning, so Black sacs the Exchange in hopes of counterplay on the a8-h1 diagonal) **28.Nxf7 Qd5** (Maybe the boy will overlook mate?!) **29.Qe4!** (This is no ordinary boy, but one of the greatest chess geniuses in history!) **29...Qd7 30.Qxe6** (The rest is a "matter of technique") **30...Qxe6 31.Rxe6 Kxf7 32.Ree1 Kg6 33.Rc7 Bf3 34.Bb2 h5 35.Rxa7 Rc8 36.Rc1 Re8 37.Ra6 h4 38.g4 Bxg4 39.Rxb6 Re2 40.Bc3 h3 41.d5 Nh4 42.Rxf6+ Kh5 43.b6 Nf3+ 44.Rxf3 Bxf3 45.b7 Re8 46.Be5! Rxe5 47.b8=Q Re4 48.Qg3 Rg4 49.d6 Black Resigns.**

Game 96
Nevednichy-J. Horvath
Odorheiu Secuiesc 1993

1.e4 c5 2.Nf3 e6 3.d3 Nc6 4.g3 d5 5.Nbd2 Bd6 6.Bg2 Nge7 7.0-0 0-0 8.Nh4 (A move originally popularized by Fischer. The idea is to rapidly throw forward the f-pawn to gain space on the Kingside, as a prelude to a later attack there) **8...Qc7** (Worth consideration is 8...Be5!? 9.f4 Bf6 as in Zuckerman-Vasyukov, Polanica Zdroi 1972. For 8...Bd7 see Game 99) **9.f4 f6 10.c3 Bd7 11.Nb3!?**

(see next diagram)

(A new try here. White wants to play Be3 and d4; but Black's next forestalls this) **11...d4! 12.c4 a6 13.Bd2 Rab8 14.Rc1** (Stopping 14...b5) **14...Be8 15.Qe2?!** (Nevednichy, whose commentary on this game we shall be referring to on several occasions, criticizes this. He recommends 15.g4! Bf7 [15...g5? is met by 16.e5!] 16.e5! [A fine thematic pawn sac

After 11.Nb3?!

to clear e4 for White's pieces] 16...fxe5 17.f5 e4! 18.Bxe4 Bxh2+ 19.Kh1 and despite the pawn minus, White has good chances for attack) **15...Bf7 16.Nf3?!** (Again g4 is promising) **16...e5!** (Reinforcing his center and stopping possibilities of the clearance sac e4-e5) **17.f5 b5** (Now Black's Queenside play holds more weight than White's Kingside possibilities) **18.Rc2** (On 18.cxb5 Rxb5 and ...a5-a4 is strong) **18...a5 19.g4 a4 20.Nc1 Qa7 21.g5?!** (21.Kh1!) **21...Nb4 22.Bxb4 cxb4 23.gxf6 gxf6 24.cxb5** (On 24.b3 bxc4! since 25.dxc4? allows 25...d3+ while on 25.bxc4 b3 is good. The first variation shows why 21.Kh1! was better) **24...b3! 25.axb3 axb3 26.Rd2 Bb4 27.Rdd1 Rxb5?!** (Better was 27...Rfc8! with the idea of ...Rc2) **28.Kh1 Rc5 29.Qf2 Kh8 30.Qh4 Qb6 31.Rg1 Rc2 32.Bh3 Qc6** (Better 32...Qd6!) **33.Rdf1 Rg8** (After 33...Rxb2? Nevednichy gives the brilliant line 34.Qh6 Rg8 35.Nxe5!! fxe5 36.Rxg8+ Bxg8 37.f6 Nf5 38.Bxf5 Qc7 39.Rg1 and White wins) **34.Qh6 Qd6!** (To stop the Knight sac on e5 seen in the above variation) **35.Bg4 Rxb2 36.Bh5 Bxh5 37.Qxh5 Qd8?** (After defending well, Black falters in time pressure. Correct was 37...Rb1! 38.Nxb3 [or 38.Qf7 b2 39.Rxg8+ Nxg8 40.Rg1 Qf8] 38...Rxb3 39.Qf7 Rxd3 and Black comes out on top) **38.Nxb3 Rxb3? 39.Qf7** (Threatening both 40.Qxf6+ mating, as well as 40.Qxb3) **39...Nd5 40.exd5 Rxg1+ 41.Rxg1 Qf8 42.Qh5 Qd8!** (To answer 43.Nh4 with 43...Qxd5+) **43.Qf7 Qf8 44.Qe6!** (Threatening 45.Nxe5!) **44...Rb2** (On 44...Bd6 45.Nd2! and Ne4) **45.Nxe5 Bd6!** (A

sneaky resource. Now the apparently winning 46.Qxd6!?? [to answer
46...Qxd6 with 47.Nf7#.] allows the brilliant shot 46...Rxh2+!! as after
47.Kxh2 Qxd6 the Ne5 is pinned and it is Black who would win!)
46.Ng4! Rc2 (On 46...h5 47.Rc1 and the threat of Rc8 defuses Black's
valiant defense) **47.Rb1 Be7 48.Re1 Bb4 49.Re4! h5 50.Nxf6 Rc1+
51.Kg2 Qg7+ 52.Kh3** (Now White's King is safe and the rest is easy)
**52...Rf1 53.Qe8+ Bf8 54.Qxh5+ Qh6 55.Qxh6+ Bxh6 56.Rg4 Bg7
57.Rh4+ Black Resigns.**

Game 97
Heissler-Wegener
German League 1994

　　**1.e4 c5 2.Nf3 Nc6 3.d3 e6 4.g3 d5 5.Nbd2 Bd6 6.Bg2 Nge7 7.0-0
0-0 8.Re1 Rb8** (Black intends to obtain play by ...b5 and ...b4) **9.c3 b5
10.e5** (But White has obtained the classic pawn outpost on e5, which all
KIA devotees know will normally give good chances of attack on the
Kingside) **10...Bc7 11.Nb3 Bb6 12.Bf4 a5 13.d4!**

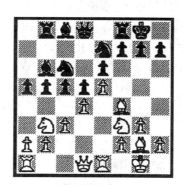

(Consolidating his hold on the center) **13...c4?!** (After 13...cxd4 14.cxd4
White is better, but the text closes off lines and is too slow versus White's
"standardized" Kingside buildup) **14.Nbd2 Bd7 15.Nf1 b4 16.a4 Bc7**
(16...bxa3 e.p. 17.Rxa3 – with Ra2 as a resource to defend b2 – also
favors White) **17.h4** (The characteristic thrust of the h-pawn, with ideas
of h5-h6 in mind) **17...f6** (Black is rightly concerned about the steady

increase of pressure against his Kingside. But this attempt to fight back there only creates further weaknesses on the Kingside) **18.exf6 Rxf6** (Since this leaves e5 as an outpost for White's pieces, he should have tried 18...gxf6 though then 19.Bxc7 Qxc7 20.Bh3 is troublesome) **19.Bxc7 Qxc7 20.N1h2 Rbf8 21.Ng4 Rf5 22.Qe2 Bc8 23.Ng5 Nd8 24.f4** (White has achieved a winning bind) **24...Nec6 25.Ne3!** (Winning material by force) **25...R5f6 26.Qc2 g6 27.Ng4 Rf5 28.Nh6+ Kh8 29.Nxf5 gxf5 30.Re3 Qg7 31.Rae1 h6 32.Nxe6!** (This return of material expedites the win) **32...Bxe6 33.Rxe6 Nxe6 34.Rxe6 Qxg3 35.Qf2 Qxf2+ 36.Kxf2 bxc3 37.bxc3 Rc8** (Black's pawns are hopelessly weak) **38.Bxd5 Nb4** (A desperate measure which White cleverly turns aside) **39.cxb4 c3 40.bxa5** (Or 40.Re1, but the text is more entertaining) **40...c2 41.Re1 c1=Q 42.Rxc1 Rxc1 43.a6 Rc7 44.Bb7! Black Resigns.**

Game 98
Dolmatov-Lautier
Polanica Zdroi 1991

1.e4 c5 2.Nf3 e6 3.d3 Nc6 4.g3 d5 5.Nbd2 Bd6 6.Bg2 Nge7 7.0-0 0-0 8.Nh4 b6 9.f4 dxe4?! (This only hands over control of the central e4 to White. Better was the restrained 9...f6 or the blockading 9...f5, though the latter leaves e5 somewhat vulnerable after 10.exd5! exd5 11.c3 followed by Ndf3 and a later d3-d4 and Ne5) **10.dxe4 Ba6 11.Re1 Bc7** (For 11...c4 see Game 100) **12.c3!**

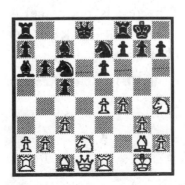

(White doesn't mind the apparent weakening of d3 as Black has no concrete way to exploit this; meanwhile, White's use of e4 [after e4-e5] will bring strong pressure to bear on Black's Kingside) **12...Bd3 13.e5 Qd7** (Black's hopes on the d-file will prove to be illusory. The right path was 13...b5 with the idea of ...c4, ...Bb6 and ...Nd5, leading to a playable game for Black. Dolmatov) **14.Ne4 Rad8 15.Qg4!** (Already threatening 16.Nf6+. So Black swaps off the Knight; but the replacement Bishop will also be an unpleasant customer) **15...Bxe4?!** (15...Kh8!?. Dolmatov) **16.Bxe4 Ng6 17.Nf3** (Suddenly it is apparent that Black has nothing at all on the d-file while White's Kingside pressure is indeed very real) **17...Nce7 18.Bc2!** (Clearing e4 for the other Knight) **18...Nf5 19.Ng5 Rfe8** (19...h6? 20.Nxe6! Nxe5 21.Nxf8) **20.Qh5 Nh6** (20...Nf8 21.g4 g6 22.Qh3 followed by 23.Ne4 is no fun either. Also, after 20...h6 21.Nxe6 Nxe5 22.Qxf5 g6 23.Qe4 Rxe6 24.fxe5 Rxe5 25.Qxe5 Bxe5 26.Rxe5 Re8 27.Rxe8+ Qxe8 28.Kf2! [not 28.Bxh6 allowing 28...Qe2] with White clearly on top. Dolmatov) **21.h4 b5 22.Kh2 b4 23.Qe2 Nf5 24.h5 Nf8 25.Ne4! Qc6 26.g4 Ne7 27.h6** (Threatening 28.hxg7 and 29.Nf6) **27...Nd7 28.hxg7 Kxg7 29.Kg3!** (Clearing the h-file for attack) **29...Ng6 30.Be3?!** (Correct was 30.g5 first and then Be3. Dolmatov) **30...bxc3 31.bxc3 Ndxe5!?** (The only way to resist) **32.fxe5 Bxe5+ 33.Kh3! f5 34.Ng3 Kh8 35.Nh5 Bxc3?!** (35...Rg8!? had to be tried) **36.Bg5 Rb8 37.Rab1 Bxe1 38.Rxe1** (Black's dark-squares are too weak to allow a good defense to White's swarming minor pieces) **38...c4 39.Bf6+ Kg8 40.Bc3 Kf7 41.Rf1** (The rest is gruesome) **41...Qc5 42.Qd2 Qe7 43.Bxf5! Qh4+** (Or 43...exf5 44.Rxf5+ Kg8 45.Qd5+ Qe6 46.Nf6+ Kf7 47.Nxe8+) **44.Kg2 Rbd8 45.Bxe6+! Ke7** (45...Kxe6 46.Ng7+ Ke7 47.Bb4+ and mate next) **46.Bb4+ Black Resigns.**

Game 99
Vasjukov-Krasenkov
St.Petersburg 1994

1.e4 c5 2.Nf3 e6 3.d3 d5 4.Nbd2 Nc6 5.g3 Bd6 6.Bg2 Nge7 7.0-0 0-0 8.Nh4 Bd7 9.f4 f5 10.c4!? (Playable, but we like 10.exd5! exd5 11.c3 followed by Ndf3, with a later d3-d4 and Ne5) **10...b5?!** (Krasenkov- whose notes we will be frequently using – gives 10...d4 with equality. We agree) **11.cxd5!** (Opening up the center allows White to take the initiative) **11...exd5 12.exf5 Nb4 13.Ndf3!**

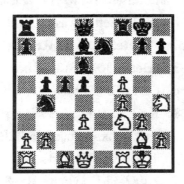

(Now 13...Nxf5 14.a3 Nc6 15.Nxf5 Bxf5 16.Ng5 slightly favors White as d5 and e6 are weak) **13...c4 14.dxc4 Bc5+ 15.Kh1 dxc4! 16.Ng5** (After 16.Ne5 Bxf5! 17.Nxf5 Nxf5 18.Bxa8 Qxa8+ 19.Qf3 Qxf3+ 20.Nxf3 Nd3 the powerfully posted Nd3 and the idea of Re8-e2 give Black very good compensation) **16...Nxf5!** (Play now enters a phase of tactical thrust and counterthrust. Now on 17.Bd5+ Kh8 18.Nxh7 [or 18.Qh5 Nh6, answering the "brilliant" 19.Qg6 with the winning retort 19...Bf5!] 18...Nxd5! [not 18...Kxh7? 19.Qh5+ Nh6 20.Be4+ and 21.Qxc5] 19.Nxf8 Bc6 gives Black dangerous counterthreats) **17.Bd2!!** (Now on 17...Bc6? White plays 18.Bxb4! [not 18.Ne6 Nxh4! 19.Bxc6 Qc8!] 18...Bxg2+ 19.Nxg2 Qxd1 [19...Bxb4 20.Qf3 leaves White well on top] 20.Raxd1 Bxb4 21.Ne6 Rf7 22.g4 and Black's Nf5 is driven back while White's Ne6 hamstrings Black's position) **17...Nxh4! 18.Bxb4**

Bxb4 (18...Nxg2? 19.Qd5+ and Bxc5) **19.Qd5+ Kh8 20.gxh4 Qe7?**
(Better was 20...Qe8! and on 21.a3 Ba5 22.Nf7+ Qxf7) **21.a3 Ba5**
22.Nf7? (Obvious but not best. Right was 22.Nxh7! Kxh7 [22...Rfc8
23.Ng5!] 23.Be4+ Qxe4+ [on 23...Kh8 24.Qh5+ Kg8 25.Bh7+ Kh8
26.Bg6+ mates; or, 23...Kh6 24.Rg1!; or, 23...g6 24.Qh5+ Kg8
25.Qxg6+ Qg7 – if 25...Kh8 26.Qh6+ Kg8 27.Rg1+ mates – 26.Qh5 Rf5
27.Qf3 wins for White.] 24.Qxe4+ Bf5 25.Qg2 Rae8 26.Rf3 Be4 Rg1
wins for White. Based on Vasjukov's notes) **22...Qxf7 23.Qxf7 Rxf7**
24.Bxa8 (White is the Exchange ahead, but Black's 3 to 2 Queenside
majority, two Bishops, and targets on b2, f4, and h4 give decent counterplay) **24...Bf5 25.Rf3 Rf8?!** (Better was 25...Re7, stopping Re3 while
planning Re2) **26.Bc6 a6 27.Re3 Bb6 28.Re7 Bc5?!** (Better 28...Bd4)
29.Rb7 Bd4 30.Re1 h5?! (Better 30...h6) **31.Rbe7??** (A terrible blunder.
Right was 31.a4! and if 31...Bxb2 then 32.axb5 axb5 33.Rxb5 c3
34.Rxf5! Rxf5 35.Re8+ Kh7 36.Be4 g6 37.Bxf5 gxf5 38.Rc8 with a
winning endgame. Better is 31...bxa4 but after 32.Bxa4 White would be
in control) **31...Bxb2** (Of course. Now Black has turned the tables)
32.Re8? Rxe8 (Not 32...Kg8? 33.Bd5+) **33.Rxe8+ Kh7 34.Be4 Bxe4**
35.Rxe4 c3 White Resigns.

Game 100
Fischer-Ivkov
Piatigorsky Cup 1966

   1.e4 c5 2.Nf3 e6 3.d3 Nc6 4.g3 d5 5.Nbd2 Bd6 6.Bg2 Nge7 7.0-0
0-0 8.Nh4 (This was the inaugural game for this move) **8...b6 9.f4 dxe4?!**
(A strategically dubious decision. After this trade of pawns White will
obtain access to the e4 square for his pieces) **10.dxe4 Ba6 11.Re1 c4**
(For 11...Bc7 – which is hardly an improvement for Black – refer back
to Game 98. The text has a fairly subtle positional idea – to sacrifice the
c-pawn by 12...c3!, as after 13.bxc3 White's doubled isolated c-pawns
would be excellent compensation for the minus pawn. But Fischer is well
aware and promptly stops this idea)

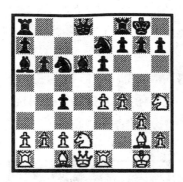

12.c3! Na5 (Probably hoping to "parachute" the Knight into d3 by Nb7-c5-d3. But this idea cannot be implemented as Fischer seizes the initiative and never gives Black time to organize any significant counterplay) **13.e5!** (Clearing the e4-square for use) **13...Bc5+ 14.Kh1 Nd5 15.Ne4** (White pieces will use the central e4-square as a transit point, on their way to "visit" the Black King's fortress) **15...Bb7 16.Qh5 Ne7** (Rushing back to try to defend) **17.g4!** (Now f5-f6 is a threat) **17...Bxe4** (To remove the menacing Knight, but the KB on e4 will also prove to be an able attacking piece) **18.Bxe4 g6** (After 18...h6 19.f5 the threat of f6 is very strong) **19.Qh6 Nd5 20.f5** (Threatening 21.f6, but also setting up a sacrificial breakthrough) **20...Re8** (To meet 21.f6 with 21...Bf8) **21.fxg6 fxg6 22.Nxg6!** (Now after 22...hxg6 23.Qxg6+ Kf8 24.Bh6+ Ke7 25.Qg7#) **22...Qd7 23.Nf4 Rad8 24.Nh5 Kh8 25.Nf6 Nxf6 26.exf6 Rg8** (Or 26...Bf8 27.Qh5 with the strong threat 28.f7, which would threaten both the Re8 as well as mate on h7) **27.Bf4** (Fischer's attack has flowed in a series of simple, natural, efficient moves. The result, when viewed afterwards, seems to have possessed an air of inevitability) **27...Rxg4 28.Rad1 Rdg8!?** (With the idea of 29.Rxd7?? Rg1+ mating) **29.f7!** (Finishing matters as 29...Qxf7 30.Be5+ and no matter what piece is interposed, 31.Qxh7# follows) **Black Resigns.**

Game 101
Yudasin-Luther
Leningrad 1989

1.e4 e6 2.d3 d5 3.Nd2 c5 4.Ngf3 Nc6 5.g3 Bd6 6.Bg2 Nge7 7.0-0 0-0 8.Re1 Bc7 9.c3 d4!? 10.Nb3 b6 11.e5 Rb8 12.cxd4 cxd4 13.Bg5 (13.h4!?) 13...Re8! 14.Rc1 Bb7 15.Rc4 (15.g4!?)

15...b5 16.Rc1 h6! 17.Nc5!? Ba8 18.Na6 hxg5 19.Nxg5 g6 20.Qg4 Bxe5! 21.Qh3 Bg7 22.Nxb8 Qxb8 23.Rxe6 fxe6! 24.Qxe6+ Kh8 25.Qh3+ Draw.

Game 102
Zapata-Lautier
Novi Sad Olympiad 1990

1.e4 e6 2.d3 d5 3.Nd2 c5 4.Ngf3 Nc6 5.g3 Bd6 6.Bg2 Nge7 7.0-0 0-0 8.Re1 f6 9.c3 Qc7 10.a3 Bd7 11.Qe2 Rac8 12.Nb3 Qb6 13.Nbd2 Kh8 14.Bh3 Qc7 15.b4

(see next diagram)

15...e5 16.Bxd7 Qxd7 17.b5 Nd8 18.c4 dxe4 19.Nxe4 Ne6 20.Bb2 Bc7 21.Nh4 Rcd8 22.Rad1 g5 23.Ng2 Ng6 24.Qh5 Qg7 25.Kh1 Rd7 26.h4 gxh4 27.Nxh4 Nxh4 28.Qxh4 f5 29.Nc3 Rf6 30.Nd5 Rh6 31.Nxc7 Rxh4+ 32.gxh4 Nd4 33.Ne6 Qg4 34.Bxd4 cxd4 White Resigns.

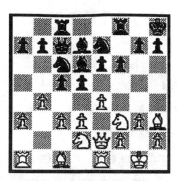

After 15.b4

Game 103
Vaganian-Sokolov
Minsk 1986

1.Nf3 c5 2.g3 d5 3.Bg2 Nc6 4.0-0 e6 5.d3 Bd6 6.e4 Nge7 7.Re1 0-0 8.Nbd2 Bc7 9.c3 a5 10.a4 b6 11.exd5 exd5 12.Nb1! Bg4 13.Na3 d4 14.Nb5 dxc3 15.bxc3 Rc8 16.Ba3 Qd7 17.d4! cxd4 18.Bxe7! Nxe7 19.Qxd4 Qxd4 20.cxd4 Nd5 21.Rac1 Bb8

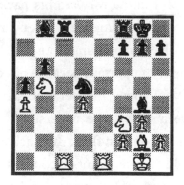

22.Ne5 Bxe5 23.Bxd5 Bf6 24.Bc6! Rfd8 25.f3?? (25.d5 Bf3 26.Rc4! Bg5 27.Nd4! Bh5 28.f4 Bf6 29.Nb5 +-) 25...Be6 26.d5 **Draw.**

CHAPTER FOUR

The KIA vs. the French

The Evolution of Bobby Fischer's Treatment of the King's Indian Attack, by GM Alexander Chernin.

The basis of this article is four of Fischer's games. Fischer-Feuerstein 1957, Bisguier-Fischer 1963, Fischer-Miagmarsuren 1967 and Nickolich-Fischer 1968.

Fischer played many more games with the KIA, but these other examples can be recognized as exceptions to his "classical" treatment of this opening. The most popular system against the KIA in Fischer's time was the French System (1.e4 e6 2.d3 d5 3.Nd2 Nf6 4.Ngf3 c5 5.g3 Nc6 6.Bg2 Be7 7.0-0 0-0. Note that this position can be obtained by transposition in several ways: e.g., 1.e4 c5 2.Nf3 e6 3.d3, etc.; or 1.Nf3 d5 2.g3 Nf6 3.Bg2 e6, etc.). From this starting point both sides general strategies became clear: Black will throw forward his pawns on the Queenside, while White will try to build a Kingside attack by moves like Nbd2, Re1, e5, Nf1, h4, and Bf4. The "tempo game" (i.e., the efficient utilization of every move) became very important because of concrete ideas on both flanks. But even the very young Fischer paid serious attention to what happened on his Queen's flank; he understood that White cannot let Black have absolute sway on that flank. If Black could do as he pleased there then White would at some point be compelled to shift some of his Kingside pieces back to the Queenside for defense. This, of course, would seriously impede White's ambitions against Black's Kingside. Specifically, the march of Black's a-pawn (a5-a4-a3) would give very good chances on the Queenside since his Nc6 could find a fine outpost on b4 without fear of White's a2-a3; the a2-pawn would be a permanent target in this case. Also (after Black's a4-a3), White would suffer from a permanent weakness on the dark-squares, since the White b2-pawn would be forced to either move up to b3 – or, even worse, capture with bxa3. Fischer's great discovery involved playing a2-a3, just before Black's a4-pawn could advance to a3. Another move which Fischer used often was c2-c4. This must be properly timed as sometimes Black might be able to favorably open the d-file with ...dxc4. Nonetheless, Fischer showed that, at the right moment, c2-c4 could be used to pressure Black's center and/or suppress Black's Queenside pawn strategies (e.g., If White's c-pawn were on c3, and Black's b-pawn pushed from b5 to b4, then c3-c4 would stop Black from being able to open the b-file by ...bxc3). The main idea of c4 is to induce the advance d5-d4; consequently, the central e4-square could be an important factor in increasing the pressure on Black's position – especially the Kingside. Summarizing: the young Fischer understood that some prophylactic measures created the most efficient path to Kingside success.

In the game with Feuerstein, after the prophylactic c2-c4, Fischer pushed the h-pawn to the h6-square to provoke ...g7-g6. The next part of the plan was to exchange Bishops on g5, to maximally weaken the dark-squares, especially f6. This was not yet enough for full success on the Kingside because of the limited maneuvering space there. Unexpectedly, Fischer decided to play on the Queenside, to lure Black's Queen to the defense of the Queenside. Then he started up again on the Kingside, with eventual success. But even this game showed the problems in this style of attack, because Fischer had to use the whole board since there was not enough space for immediately decisive actions on the Kingside.

The next game vs. Bisguier brought him more problems, partly because Fischer was a tempo down (he played Black). When Fischer played ...h5-h4-h3, Bisguier played B(e2)-f1 to stop the exchange of Bishops (and consequently avoided the weakening of vital Kingside squares – as seen in the Feuerstein game). This circumstance caused Fischer to just wait. Later, he used some mistakes by Bisguier – who opened lines improperly on the Queenside – to achieve the victory. But, it was obviously not a satisfying result from the opening. Therefore, a better attacking method was sought. Fischer eschewed the h-pawn march to h6 (or, as Black, to h3), instead leaving it on h4 (h5) for piece moves like Ng5 or Bg5; also, the h5-square was left free for his Queen. Fischer used these new ideas to perfection to achieve a stronger Kingside attack (he still continued with the prophylactic measure a2-a3 on the Queenside). In the game Fischer-Miagmarsuren, Black played purposefully and well. He completely destroyed White's Queenside and center, but White's attack was still stronger, resulting in mate in the nick of time.

In the game Nikolich-Fischer, Black successfully used the g4-square (in this case by means of a beautiful sacrificial motif). Generally these last two examples show how Fischer's viewpoint substantially evolved. Additional examples are Fischer-Ivkov, where Black opened the d-file at a poor time; or Fischer-U.Geller, when Fischer opened the e-file with the typical sacrificial motif Bxd5 and e5-e6. Also, in Fischer-Durao, Black's defective pawn moves on the Queenside (...b6 & ...a5) were exploited with great skill. But such games are somewhat exceptional to our earlier stated "classical" main lines.

Game 104
Fischer-Feuerstein
U.S. Championship 1957

1.e4 c5 2.Nf3 e6 3.g3 Nf6 4.d3 d5 5.Nbd2 Be7 6.Bg2 O-O 7.O-O Nc6 8.Re1 Qc7 (Current theory recognizes 8...b5 as the preferred move. However, 8...Qc7 induces White to play Qe2, in order to properly reinforce the advance e4-e5) **9.Qe2 Rd8 10.e5 Ne8** (Black's last two moves were not so good, limiting his chances of attack on the Queenside; better was 10...Nd7) **11.c3** (Also reasonable was 11.h4) **11...b5 12.Nf1 b4 13.Bf4 Qa5** (Better was 13...bxc3) **14.c4!** (Closing lines on the Queenside while the opening of the d-file by ...dxc4 doesn't give Black anything substantial) **14...Nc7 15.h4 Qb6 16.h5 b3** (Black is trying to isolate White's c-pawn in order to later attack it by moves like ...dxc4,

...Ba6, coupled with ...Rac8 and ...Nd4, hoping to play on the c-file after Nxd4 cxd4. It is amazing that White, not Black, is able to later benefit from the position of the b3-pawn) **17.a3 dxc4 18.dxc4 Ba6 19.N1h2 Rac8** (Too slow; better was 19...Nd4) **20.h6 g6 21.Bg5** (Because of the position of the Rd8, Black cannot avoid the trade of dark-squared Bishops by Bf8. Compare this situation with Game 105: Bisguier-Fischer) **21...Nd4 22.Qe3 Bxg5 23.Qxg5 Ne8 24.Ng4 Nf5 25.Rac1 Qc7** (On the Kingside, Black is saddled with chronically weak squares at f6, g5 and g7. But White does not yet have enough potential to utilize these weaknesses. For example, 26.Nf6+? Nxf6 27.Qxf6 Nxh6. However, the next sequence of moves by White is designed to finesse the Black Queen away from using the e7-square for defense – "facing-off" the invading Qg5, while the Nf5 will also be eventually undermined in order to remove its control of g7 and h6) **26.Nd2!** (Now 26...Qe7 is not possible because the b3-pawn would fall) **26...Rd4 27.Nxb3 Rxc4 28.Rcd1! Ra4** (Again, not 28...Qe7 because of 29.Qxe7 Nxe7 30.Ne3 Ra4 31.Rd7) **29.Re4!**

29...Bb5 (After 29...Rxe4 30.Bxe4 Qe7 31.Qxe7 Nxe7 32.Rd7 White wins. But, a much more challenging defense is 30...Be2. Yet the young Fischer had seen a complicated and by no means obvious solution: 31.Bxf5!! Bxd1 [31...exf5 32.Nf6+ Nxf6 33.Qxf6 Kf8 34.Nxc5! Qxc5 35.Rd8+ Rxd8 36.Qxd8#] 32.Nf6+ Kh8 [32...Nxf6 33.Qxf6 Kf8

34.Bxe6 Bxb3 35.Qg7+ Ke8 36.Qg8+ Ke7 37.Qxf7+ Kd8 38.Qf8#; or, 32...Kf8 33.Nxh7+ Kg8 34.Nf6+ Kf8 35.h7 Kg7 36.h8=Q+! Kxh8 37.Qh6#] 33.Nxe8 Qd8! 34.Qxd8 Rxd8 35.Nd6 Kg8 [35...Rxd6 36.exd6 Bxb3 37.d7] 36.Bxe6! fxe6 37.Nxc5 and White must win. For example, 37...Bg4 38.Nce4 and Nf6 will be deadly) **30.Rc1! Qb6** (After all, the Black Queen has been diverted from e7 and as a result the White attack will finally break through to Black's King) **31.Nd2 Rxe4 32.Nxe4 Bd3** (The ending after 32.Qd8 is hopeless) **33.Ngf6+ Kh8 34.g4** (Now the main defender of Black's fortress is knocked-out, and the battle is over) **34...Bxe4 35.Bxe4 Nd4 36.Nxe8 Qd8 37.Qxd8 Rxd8 38.Nd6 Ne2+ 39.Kf1 Nxc1 40.Nxf7+ Kg8 41.Nxd8 Nb3 42.Ke2 Nd4+ 43.Kd3 Kf8 44.Nc6 Black Resigns.**

A great game! But the difficulties involved with the attack were obvious in this game. I think that Fischer realized that even more clearly after the next game. His opponent, Bisguier, avoided the exchange of the white-squared Bishops; after this, Fischer could only wait until Bisguier played poorly in the center, giving Fischer the chance to hit him with 34...Nxh2. After this game it became clear that the Kingside attack pattern with the h-pawn moving forward to h6 (or h3, from Black's perspective) left the position too closed to obtain an ongoing attack. So in the following years Fischer left his pawn on h4 (h5), using its position as a support point for Ng5 or Bg5 (sometimes even with a sacrifice – see Nickolich-Fischer); also, the h5-square was available for the Queen.

Game 105
Bisguier-Fischer
Western Open 1963

1.d4 Nf6 2.c4 g6 3.Nc3 Bg7 4.Nf3 0-0 5.e3 d6 6.Be2 Nbd7 7.0-0 e5 8.b4 Re8 9.Bb2 e4 10.Nd2 Nf8 11.Qc2 Bf5 12.d5 (The usual plan here begins with 12.a4) **12...h5 13.Nb5 h4 14.Nd4 Bd7 15.a3?** (Better was 15.Rfc1) **15...h3 16.g3 Qe7 17.Rfc1 Bg4 18.Bf1 N8h7 19.a4 Ng5 20.a5 a6** (Just as he used to do later, Fischer doesn't allow the move a5-a6 [a4-a3]. See the next game) **21.Rab1 Nd7** (In order to try to make some progress on the Kingside, Fischer needs to exchange some minor pieces) **22.c5! Bxd4 23.Bxd4 Ne5 24.Bxe5 Qxe5 25.Nc4 Qe7** (On 25...Qxd5 26.cxd6; or 25...Qf6 26.Qb2) **26.b5** (Since Black is not able to create more pressure against White's Kingside, White now takes the opportunity to press on the Queenside) **26...axb5 27.Rxb5 dxc5! 28.Rxb7 Qd8!**

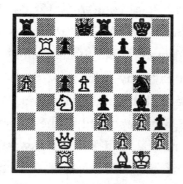

29.Qc3 (Better was 29.Qb2! and if 29...Bc8 30.Rb8) **29...Bc8 30.Rb5 Qxd5 31.Qa3 Qd8!** (The situation has changed; with the demise of the d5-pawn the defense of the f3-square is a problem as Nc4-d2 is not available) **32.Qxc5 Nf3+ 33.Kh1 Qf6 34.Qxc7?** (This is a fatal mistake; necessary was 34.Rb2 to continue the fight) **34...Nxh2! 35.Kxh2 Qxf2+ 36.Kh1 Bg4 White Resigns**.

The next game is, in my opinion, the best KIA Fischer ever played. By using the right strategy (keeping the h-pawn on h4 and using the squares g5, g4 and h5), Fischer is able to concentrate more power against the enemy King. His opponent pursues his goals with great consistency: he completely destroys White's center and Queenside and is about to win by sheer advantage in material. But in this battle of minds, Fischer's inspiration prevails: with only three pieces left on the Kingside, he creates a striking combinative finish of a type which is rarely seen in practical play.

Game 106
Fischer-Miagmarsuren
Sousse 1967

1.e4 e6 2.d3 d5 3.Nd2 Nf6 4.g3 c5 5.Bg2 Nc6 6.Ngf3 Be7 7.0-0 0-0 8.e5 Nd7 9.Re1 b5 10.Nf1 b4 11.h4 a5 (Black avoids wasting time on 11...Qc7) **12.Bf4!** (A good move, overprotecting e5 so that the Nf3 can later play to g5) **12...a4 13.a3!** (Stopping a4-a3) **13...bxa3 14.bxa3 Na5 15.Ne3** (After 15.N1h2 Black could play 15...c4 16.d4 c3 with the idea of ...Nc4) **15...Ba6 16.Bh3** (This Bishop increases the pressure on the white squares, to add more effect to the coming Ng5) **16...d4** (Since 16...c4 17.d4 doesn't have any force now, Black changes his plan: he now intends to use d5 for his Knight. However, White now has the use of e4, which will be very important in the future) **17.Nf1!** (Why not 17.Ng4?; It is more natural. But Black's pawns are on their original squares at f7, g7 and h7; also, Black's Be7 is still alive. This means that White would have difficulty successfully attacking this fortress. On the other hand I have seen an interesting game with the Knights on g4 and g5; thereafter the pattern of attack proceeded with Nh6+,...gxh6 / Nxh7!, ...Kxh7 / Qh5. Then followed Re4!, and after Black captured on e4, White retook with Bxe4, with a decisive result. However, for this type of attack, it was necessary to have the White KB on g2 instead of h3 – as played in this game. By playing 17.Nf1!, Fischer keeps the d1-h5 path available for a later Qh5. Then with Ng5, Black would be induced to advance h7-h6 [which would be undesirable because of the threats to sacrifice with B or Nxh6], or Black would have to "say goodbye" to his valuable Be7) **17...Nb6 18.Ng5 Nd5 19.Bd2** (It is not time for a sacrifice yet: 19.Qh5 h6! 20.Nxf7 Nxf4 21.Nxh6+ gxh6 22.gxf4 Kg7!) **19...Bxg5 20.Bxg5** (In the next game we are going to see Fischer even sacrifice a piece – in order to open the h-file. But in this game he does not attempt to use the h-file immediately. Really, even if he did try to use the h-file by recapturing with 20.hxg5, Black could then defend the h7-square by

...Nf8) **20...Qd7 21.Qh5 Rfc8** (Black is preparing his counterplay. However, this move may have been a reason for Black's loss. If he had played 21...Bb7 [instead of 21...Rfc8], then the later variant [seen in the note to Black's 23rd move] 23...gxf6 24.exf6 Kh8 25.Nf3! would be met by 25...Bxf3. On the other hand, the situation is getting dangerous anyway; if Black tries 21...Bb7 then he is losing support for the counterplay with ...c5-c4. However, this sort of thing becomes obvious only in the "post-mortem.") **22.Nd2 Nc3 23.Bf6 Qe8** (After 23...gxf6 24.exf6 Kh8 25.Nf3 Rg8 26.Ne5 wins) **24.Ne4 g6 25.Qg5!** (It is not time for 25.Qh6 because of 25...Qf8. So White waits while moving up other pieces) **25...Nxe4 26.Rxe4 c4** (Or 26...Bb7 27.Rg4 Qf8 [27...Qc6 28.Kh2 with the idea of Qh6] 28.h5 h6 29.Qh4 g5 30.f4 Bf3 31.fxg5 Bxg4 32.Qxg4 hxg5 33.Qxg5+ Kh7 34.Bg2 wins) **27.h5! cxd3 28.Rh4** (The first threat: 29.hxg6 fxg6 30.Rxh7!) **28...Ra7** (Another possibility was 28...Rc7 [in order to not block the 7th rank after ...Bb7], though then White has 29.Bxe6 fxe6 [forced] 30.hxg6 Qxg6 31.Qxg6+ hxg6 32.Rh8+ Kf7 33.Rh7+ Ke8 34.Rxc7 winning)

29.Bg2!! dxc2 (Or 29...Bb7 30.hxg6 fxg6 31.Rxh7) **30.Qh6 Qf8** (30...c1=Q+ 31.Rxc1 Rxc1+ 32.Kh2! wins in the same beautiful manner as the actual game) **31.Qxh7+! Black Resigns** (The variant 31...Kxh7 32.hxg6+ Kxg6 33.Be4# reminds one of a "photo-finish").

In the next game, the "short-side" castling of the White King – in conjunction with the weaknesses arising from the early pawn advances g3 and h3- becomes a basis for a brilliant attack. Fischer, by using the position of his h5-pawn, finds a spectacular piece sacrifice whose object is to force open the h-file; then White is unable to stem the following invasion of Black's Queen.

Game 107
Nickolich-Fischer
Vinkovci 1968

1.c4 g6 2.Nc3 Bg7 3.g3 e5 4.Bg2 d6 5.e3 Nf6! 6.Nge2 0-0 7.0-0 c6 8.d4 Re8 9.Rab1 e4 10.b4 Bf5 11.h3 h5 12.Nf4 Nbd7 13.a4 Nf8 14.c5? d5 (Now Black's center is very firm, allowing freedom of action for a buildup against White's weakened Kingside) 15.b5 N8h7 16.Bd2 Ng5 17.Rb2 Qd7 18.Kh2 Bh6!

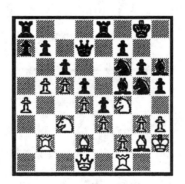

(An even more inspired idea than we saw in the previous game. This move not only clears the way for ...Kg7 and ...Rh8, but also targets the Nf4, which is one of the very few defenders of the White Kingside) 19.a5 Bg4! 20.hxg4 hxg4 21.Rh1 Nf3+ 22.Bxf3 gxf3 23.Kg1 Bxf4 24.exf4 Kg7 (White has no defense to the following invasion down the h-file) 25.f5 Rh8 26.Bh6+ Rxh6 27.Rxh6 Kxh6 28.Qd2+ g5 29.bxc6 Qf5 30.Nd1 Qh3 31.Ne3 Kg6 (32...Ng4 will mate quickly)**White Resigns.**

Of course, Fischer played a number of other games in the KIA opening. In many of them he took advantage of his opponent's mistakes in a masterly fashion. All of these games can teach a lot. I've chosen those games in which the pattern of play is mostly "visually" impressive. But my main thought was to describe the evolution of Fischer's points of view about different methods of attack in this system.

CHAPTER FIVE

A BRIEF SURVEY OF VARIOUS OTHER DEFENSES

Game 108
Vujadinovic-B. Ivanovic
Cetinje 1993

1.e4 c5 2.d3 Nc6 3.g3 d5 4.Nd2 Nf6 5.Bg2 g6 6.Ngf3 Bg7 7.0-0 0-0

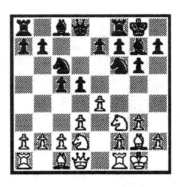

(Black has adopted the Classical Fianchetto Variation – a tempo down. This designation comes from White's line against the King's Indian Defense: i.e., 1.d4 Nf6 2.c4 g6 3.g3 Bg7 4.Bg2 0-0 5.Nf3 d6 6.0-0 Nbd7 7.Nc3 e5. Since the colors are inverted in our game, a good way to describe the situation is that White is playing a King's Indian "Defense" – but has a full extra move. Since the King's Indian Defense is perfectly good for Black, some might think that with a whole "extra" move this form of the KIA would automatically give White a definite advantage. Actually, theory gives Black approximately even chances. But this evaluation is tempered by the cautionary note that if Black "forgets" he is a tempo down, that is, tries to push for the initiative too hard, then he can certainly run into trouble. So with White the Classical Fianchetto against the King's Indian Defense should allow White a slight plus; but with Black, if it is played accurately it can equalize – but no more than that) **8.c3 b6 9.Re1** (Reserving options of both e4-e5 as well as exd5.

The first course gains space, but closes up the position to some extent. The second course is more active in the sense that it opens lines [the h1-a8 diagonal as well as the e-file]. Often the choice of plans is simply a matter of style more than any objective considerations) **9...dxe4** (Although this is playable, there is a germ of possible trouble in the fact that by exchanging off the d5-pawn, the e4-square can sometimes be used by White's pieces [after e4-e5]. The continuation 9...e5 is possible though after 10.exd5 Nxd5 11.Nc4 White has good play against Black's pawn center) **10.dxe4 Bb7?!** (Better was 10...Ng4) **11.e5** (As usual the push of the e-pawn to e5 allows White to claim the initiative) **11...Ne8 12.Qa4!** (A forceful idea. The White Queen is headed for the Black Kingside to stir up attacking chances) **12...Qc8 13.Qh4 Nc7 14.Ne4!** (White's minor pieces are suddenly headed for the Kingside. The tactical basis is simple: 14...Nxe5? loses to 15.Nxe5 Bxe5 16.Ng5 threatening mate and Rxe5) **14...Ne6 15.Bh6! Rd8 16.Bh3!** (A very annoying pin. Now poor is 16...Nxe5 17.Nxe5 Bxe5 18.Qxe7 with a winning position) **16...Bxe5 17.Nfg5** (All four of White's minor pieces join in the fun!) **17...Nxg5!?** (Hoping for 18.Bxc8? Nf3+ 19.Kf1 Bxc8! and Black wins as the White Queen is surrounded) **18.Nxg5 e6** (Forced. After 18...Qc7 White strikes with 19.Nxf7! as 19...Kxf7 gets mated after 20.Qc4+) **19.Bg7!** (Also winning is 19.Nxh7!. After White's shift of all four of his pieces to the Kingside, it is not very surprising that there is more than one way to a sacrificial victory) **19...Bxg7** (On 19...Kxg7 20.Qxh7+ Kf6 21.Qxf7+ Kxg5 22.Rxe5+! Nxe5 23.Qf4+ Kh5 24.Qh4#) **20.Qxh7+ Kf8 21.Nxe6+** (Again White has more than one way to sacrifice as 21.Rxe6! gives excellent chances of success) **21...fxe6 22.Bxe6 Qxe6** (On 22...Qc7 23.Qg8+ Ke7 24.Qxg7+ Kd6 25.Rad1+ Nd4 26.Rxd4+! cxd4 27.Qxd4+ Kc6 28.Qc4+ Kd6 29.Rd1+ wins handily) **23.Rxe6** (Black has garnered three pieces for his Queen, but the drafty position of his King combined with the advance of White's extra Kingside pawns allows White to secure the win) **23...Re8!? 24.Rae1!** (Not 24.Rxg6 Re7 with the idea of Ne5 and Black can offer real resistance) **24...Rxe6 25.Rxe6 Rd8 26.f4!** (Taking e5 away from Black's pieces and preparing to advance further with f4-f5 after White snaps off the g6-pawn) **26...Rd1+ 27.Kf2 Rd2+ 28.Ke3!** (White avoids 28.Re2? Rxe2+ as he wants to keep his Rook for attacking purposes) **28...Rd7 29.Qxg6** (With three connected passers now on White's side, the rest is easy) **29...Ne7 30.Qg5 Bd5 31.f5! Bxe6 32.fxe6 Rd5 33.Qf4+ Nf5+** (Or 33...Rf5 34.Qb8+) **34.Ke4** (White was in serious time pressure here; 34.Kf2 was easier) **34...Re5+ 35.Qxe5** (Better 35.Kd3, though the text still wins as Black can't hold back the passers) **35...Bxe5 36.Kxe5 Ne3 37.h4 Ke7 38.h5 b5 39.Kf4 Nd5+ 40.Kf5 Ne3+ 41.Kg6** (Now 41...Kxe6 42.h6 wins) **Black Resigns.**

Game 109
Reshevsky-Sherwin
New York 1954

   1.Nf3 Nf6 2.g3 g6 3.Bg2 Bg7 4.0-0 0-0 5.d3 d5 6.Nbd2 c5 7.e4 (Arriving at the "Classical Fianchetto Reversed" – as in the previous game) **7...e6** (Unusual, but playable. After 7...Nc6 and ...e5 White would have the typical King's Indian option of playing for exd5, opening up the e-file for pressure against Black's e5-pawn, and the long-diagonal from h1-a8. With 7...e6, Black is playing ultra stodgy chess. But at the same time, this restrained approach certainly is not calculated to instill fear in KIA players!) **8.Re1 Nc6**

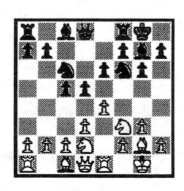

(Now the position somewhat resembles the Kasparov-Sicilian System, except that the KN is on f6 instead of e7 and Black has castled early-which, as we discussed in the early games of this book, can be hazardous to Black's health. On the other hand, with the Nf6 White cannot push e4-e5 indiscriminately as after Nfd7 the point e5 is under more pressure than usual; e.g., 9.e5?! Nd7 10.Nb3 Ndxe5 is quite convenient for Black) **9.exd5** (Another way is 9.c3 with the idea of e4-e5 and then d3-d4) **9...Nxd5** (If 9...exd5 then 10.d4! cxd4 11.Nb3 and Black will remain with an isolated d-pawn. But after 9...Nxd5, White's QN will find a good post at c4) **10.Nc4 Qc7 11.a4 Rd8?!** (This leaves the f7-square weakened, a fact which Reshevsky later turns to account) **12.Qe2** (White's plan is to establish a Knight outpost on e5) **12...b6** (On 12...Nd4 13.Nxd4 cxd4 14.a5 White retains the edge) **13.c3 h6 14.Nfe5 Nxe5 15.Nxe5 Bb7 16.a5! Ne7?** (White threatened 17.a6 Bc8 [17...Bc6 18.Nxc6 Qxc6 19.c4] 18.c4. But now White unleashes a deadly strike against the f7-square. He should have played 16...Rab8) **17.Nxf7! Kxf7** (On 17...Bxg2 18.Nxd8! Bh3 19.Ne6 wins) **18.Qxe6+ Kf8 19.Bf4 Qd7 20.Bxb7 Qxb7 21.Bd6! Rxd6 22.Qxd6** (This pin is deadly) **22...Re8 23.Ra4!** (Threatening 24.Rf4+ Kg8 25.Qe6+ and 26.Rf7) **23...g5 24.Rae4 bxa5 25.R1e3!** (White's Rooks ride rough-shod over the hapless Black position) **25...Qb6 26.Rf3+ Kg8 27.Qd7!** (Crunch!) **27...Rf8 28.Rxe7 Rxf3 29.Rxg7+ Black Resigns.**

Game 110
Stein-Moisiev
USSR Championship 1970

1.g3 d5 2.Bg2 Nf6 3.d3 g6 4.Nd2 Bg7 5.Ngf3 0-0 6.0-0 c5 7.e4 Nc6 8.exd5 Nxd5 9.Nc4 b6 10.a4 Bb7 11.a5 Rb8 12.axb6 axb6 13.c3 b5 14.Ne3 Nc7 15.Qe2 Qd7 16.Rd1

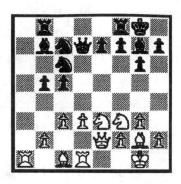

16...Ra8? (16...Ne5!?) 17.Rxa8 Rxa8 18.Ng5! e6?! 19.Ne4 Qe7 20.Ng4 f6 21.Be3 Na6 22.d4 c4 23.d5! exd5 24.Rxd5 Nc7 25.Rd1! Ne8 26.Nc5 h5 27.Nxb7 Qxb7 28.Nh6+ Kh7 29.Nf5! Rc8 30.Be4! Qf7 31.Nd6 Nxd6 32.Rxd6 Ne5 33.Qxh5+ Kg8 34.Qd1 Qe7 35.Qd5+ Kh7 36.Re6 Qd8 37.Rxe5! fxe5 38.Qe6 Rc7 39.Bb6 Qd1+ 40.Kg2 Rd7 41.Bxg6+ **Black Resigns.**

Game 111
Jansa-Forintos
Athens 1969

1.Nf3 Nf6 2.g3 c5 3.Bg2 Nc6 4.0-0 g6 5.d3 d5 6.Nbd2 Bg7 7.e4 0-0 8.Re1 h6 9.c3 dxe4 10.dxe4 Be6 11.Qe2 Qa5 12.a4 Rfd8 13.Qb5 Qb6 14.Bf1 Nd7 15.Nc4 Bxc4 16.Bxc4 Nde5 17.Nxe5 Nxe5 18.Be2 Qc7 19.Be3 Rac8 20.Red1

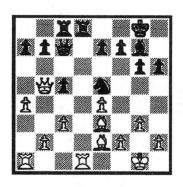

20...Rd6 21.Rxd6 exd6 22.Rd1 Rd8 23.f4 Nc6 24.Qc4 Qe7 25.Qd5 Kh7 26.Kf2 Re8 27.Bf3 Bf8 28.Rd3 a6 29.Qc4 Qf6 30.Kg2 Kg8 31.Qd5 h5 32.Bd2 Re6 33.b4 cxb4 34.cxb4 Qb2 35.Qb3 Qxb3 36.Rxb3 Bg7 37.Rd3 Kf8 38.f5 gxf5 39.exf5 Re5 40.Rd6 Rxf5 41.Bxc6 bxc6 42.Rxc6 Bd4 43.Bf4 Rf6 44.Rxf6 **Black Resigns.**

Game 112
Plachetka-Pribyl
Czechoslovakian Championship 1974

1.Nf3 Nf6 2.g3 g6 3.Bg2 Bg7 4.0-0 d5 5.d3 0-0 6.Nbd2 c5 7.e4 Nc6 8.c3 d4 9.cxd4 cxd4 10.a4 e5 11.Nc4 Ne8

12.b4 a6 13.Bd2 Nd6 14.Nxd6 Qxd6 15.b5 Ne7 16.Qb3 a5 17.Bc1 Be6 18.Qa3 Qd7 19.Ng5 Rfc8 20.Nxe6 Qxe6 21.Qb2 Bf8 22.Bd2 Rc5 23.Rac1 Nc8 24.Rxc5 Bxc5 25.Rc1 Qd6 26.Qb3 Nb6 27.f4 Bb4 28.fxe5 Qxe5 29.Bf4 Qe6 30.Qxe6 fxe6 31.Bh3 Re8 32.Rc7 Nxa4 33.Rxb7 Nc5 34.Ra7 e5 35.Bh6 a4 36.b6 Rb8 37.b7 Nxb7 38.Be6+ Kh8 39.Bd5 a3 40.Bxb7 Bc5 41.Ra6 **Black Resigns.**

Game 113
Popovic-Kirov
Wroclaw 1979

1.g3 d5 2.Bg2 Nf6 3.d3 c5 4.Nf3 g6 5.0-0 Bg7 6.Nbd2 0-0 7.e4 Nc6 8.c3 e5 9.a4 h6

10.a5!? dxe4 11.dxe4 Be6 12.Qe2 Qc7 13.a6 b6 14.Nc4 Nd7 15.Rd1
Rab8 16.Be3 b5 17.Nd6 c4 18.Nb7! Ra8 19.Nh4 Nd8 20.Nd6 Rb8
21.Nhf5! gxf5 22.exf5 Nc5 23.fxe6 fxe6 24.Nxb5! Rxb5 25.Qxc4 Rxb2
26.Qxc5 Qf7 27.Qxa7 Qf5 28.Qc5 Black Resigns.

Game 114
Shirov-Georgadze
Tbilisi 1989

    1.Nf3 d5 2.g3 Nf6 3.Bg2 c5 4.0-0 Nc6 5.d3 g6 6.Nbd2 Bg7 7.e4 0-0
8.c3 dxe4 9.dxe4 h6 10.Qe2 Be6 11.Nc4 Rc8 12.Ne1 Qd7

13.f4 (+=) 13...Rfd8 14.Ne3 Bg4 15.Nf3 Bh5 16.e5 Ne8 17.Qf2 Bxf3
18.Bxf3 e6 19.h4 h5 20.g4 hxg4 21.Bxg4 Ne7 22.h5 Nf5 23.hxg6 fxg6
24.Nxf5 exf5 25.Be2 Qf7 26.Be3 b6 27.Kh2 Nc7 28.Rg1 c4 29.Qf1
Nd5 30.Rg3 b5 31.Bd4 Bh6 32.Rh3 Qf8 33.Rh4 Bxf4+ 34.Kh1 Bg5

35.Rh2 Qg7 36.Qf3 Bf4 37.e6 Be5 38.Bxe5 Qxe5 39.Rg1 Ne7 40.Qh5 Qg7 41.Rxg6 Nxg6 42.Rg2 Rc7 43.Rxg6 Rf8 44.Rxg7+ Rxg7 45.Bf3 Rh7 46.Qxh7+ Kxh7 47.Bh5 Black Resigns.

Game 115
Botvinnik-Pomar
Varna 1962

1.g3 d5 2.Nf3 c5 3.Bg2 Nc6 4.d3 e5 5.0-0 Bd6 6.e4 (Also good is 6.Nc3 – a reversed Samisch-Panno Variation) **6...d4** (On 6...Nge7 7.Nc3 is good) **7.Nbd2 Nge7 8.c4** (Also playable is 8.c3) **8...f6** (Transposing into a reversed Samisch Variation) **9.Nh4!**

(Going for the advance f2-f4 to strive for the initiative) **9...Be6** (Of course not 9...g5? 10.Qh5+) **10.f4 exf4** (If 10...0-0, then 11.f5 Bf7 12.g4 launches the stereotyped but quite strong pawn-avalanche attack which makes the King's Indian [in this case KIA] a favorite of uncompromising players) **11.gxf4 Qc7** (Hoping to seize the attack by 0-0-0 and g7-g5. But Botvinnik has a brilliant idea up his sleeve) **12.e5!!** (A superb pawn sacrifice. The idea is to force Black to blockade his e5-square while clearing the central e4 for White's pieces. Also, the long-diagonal is opened for White's Bg2) **12...fxe5 13.f5! Bf7 14.Ne4 0-0-0 15.Qg4!** (Threatening 16.f6+ as well as 16.Qxg7. This latter pawn grab may seem to be "too risky," but the iron-clad blockade of e5 leaves Black no real attacking chances) **15...Kb8 16.Qxg7 Bh5 17.Rf2** (Black threatened

, 17...Be2) **17...h6 18.Bd2** (Even stronger seems 18.Nf6 and Black's Bh5 is in real trouble; probably Botvinnik overlooked this as he is already very satisfied with his prospects) **18...Rdg8 19.Qf6 Nc8 20.Ng6! Bxg6 21.fxg6 Be7 22.Qf7 Nd8 23.Qf5 Bh4 24.Rf3 Ne7** (Now Black will once again be a pawn up, but with a very difficult position) **25.Qh3 Nxg6 26.Nf6! Bxf6 27.Rxf6 Qe7** (After 27...Nf4 28.Bxf4 exf4 29.Rf1 Rf8 30.Rxh6 Rxh6 31.Qxh6 White is much better; the Black Knight is no match for the mighty Bishop – not to mention White's outside passed h-pawn) **28.Raf1 Nf4??** (A terrible blunder. But even after the better 28...Qg7 29.Kh1 Black is in bad shape) **29.R6xf4! exf4 30.Bxf4+** (Black now realizes that 30...Ka8 is met by 31.Qc8#) **Black Resigns.**

Game 116
Larsen-Kraidman
Manila 1974

1.g3 c5 2.Bg2 Nc6 3.Nf3 d5 4.0-0 e5 5.d3 Be7 (Entering a "Reversed Classical" Variation [the same as White's system after 1.d4 Nf6 2.c4 g6 3.Nc3 Bg7 4.e4 d6 5.Be2, etc.] except that here the KIA has that extra tempo) **6.e4** (Also good is 6.c4 d4 7.e3, a tempo-up reversed Benoni; or, 6.c4 dxc4 7.Qa4 Bd7 8.Qxc4) **6...dxe4** (Black decides to "chicken out" of the middlegame) **7.dxe4 Qxd1 8.Rxd1**

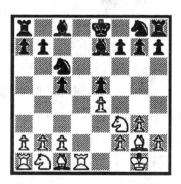

(This type of ending is, of course, well-known from the theory of the King's Indian Defense. The pawn structure actually favors White, as

Black must endure the hole at d5. Naturally, the extra tempo of the KIA can only make Black's drawing attempt more challenging. Add to this the fact that Larsen is an exceptionally strong expert in the ending, and it must seem that Kraidman was a bit optimistic in choosing 6...dxe4) **8...Bg4** (It is interesting to compare this position to the one White can obtain after 1.d4 Nf6 2.c4 g6 3.Nc3 Bg7 4.e4 d6 5.Be2 0-0 6.Nf3 e5 7.dxe5 dxe5 8.Qxd8 Rxd8 9.Bg5 [with the idea of Bxf6 and Nd5] and now if 9...Re8 then 10.0-0-0 and White has a minuscule edge [though Black should equalize with accurate play]. This is due mainly to his advanced development, which slightly outweighs the hole at d4. In the given position, however, White's extra tempo is easily put to use. With 9.c3 all threats of ...Bxf3 and ...Nd4 are nullified and Black will not be able to emulate White's Queenside castling, as in the above variant) **9.c3 Rd8** (Clearly Black is trying to trade everything off the board in order to get the coveted draw) **10.Rxd8+ Bxd8 11.Be3 b6 12.Na3!** (White will pressure Black's Queenside pawn chain) **12...Nge7 13.Nb5 Nc8** (Not 13...a6? 14.Nd6+ Kf8 and Black has only further weakened his Queenside pawns) **14.h3 Be6 15.Bf1** (The KB eyes the weakened light-squares on the left flank) **15...f6** (In order to play Kf7 to allow his Rook into play, but this creates further weakness on the light-squares) **16.Nd2** (With ideas of Bc4 – trading his KB for Black's "good" Be6) **16...a6 17.Na3 Nb8** (An amusing scenario. Black's horse must pull back as 17...a5 creates more holes at b5 and c4) **18.Nc2 Be7 19.a4** (Keeping the targets at a6 and b6 under restraint) **19...Kf7 20.h4** (Larsen once wrote a book on the advance of the Rook pawns as a component of higher level strategy!) **20...a5** (He can't stand to leave his Nb8 out of play, especially as White might engineer a break with b2-b4 at a favorable moment) **21.Bc4!** (Leaving Black with a "bad" Bishop) **21...Rd8 22.Na3** (Notice how White's Knight's beat a path toward Black's holes) **22...Nc6 23.Bxe6+ Kxe6 24.Ndc4 h5 25.Kf1 Rd7 26.Ke2 Nd8 27.Nb5** (All three of White's minor pieces clearly outshine Black's counterparts) **27...Nb7**

28.f4! (With this pawn break White turns up the heat) **28...exf4 29.gxf4 f5 30.e5 Nd8** (Trying to reach the blockade square at e6) **31.Rg1!** (Giving Black no time to maneuver) **31...Kf7 32.Nbd6+!** (Now Black's position is crumbling) **32...Nxd6 33.exd6 Bxd6 34.Rd1 Ke6 35.Nxb6** (The net result is two weakies at a5 and c5) **35...Rb7 36.Nc4 Be7 37.Bxc5!** (Simple but convincing) **37...Bxh4 38.Rd6+ Ke7** (On 38...Kf7 39.Rxd8! and 40.Nd6+ wins) **39.Nxa5 Rd7 40.Nc6+ Black Resigns.**

Game 117
Federov-Suetin
Moscow Open 1992

1.Nf3 Nf6 2.g3 c5 3.Bg2 Nc6 4.0-0 e5 5.d3 d5 6.Nbd2 Be7 7.e4 0-0 (7...d4) **8.exd5** (8.Qe2; 8.Re1) **8...Nxd5 9.Re1 f6 10.c3**

10...Nc7! (10...Be6 11.d4!) **11.Nb3?!** (Better was 11.Ne4!?; if 11...f5? then 12.Neg5 is strong for White. Also on 11...Be6 12.Be3 b6 13.d4 +=; or if 11...Bg4 12.h3 Bh5 13.Be3 b6 14.g4 Bf7 15.Ng5, again +=) **11...Bg4** (11...Bf5 12.d4, or 11...Be6 12.d4. Suetin) **12.h3 Bh5 13.Be3 b6 14.g4 Bf7 15.Nfd2** (15.Ng5 Bd5 [15...fxg5 16.Bxc6 Rb8=] 16.Ne4 is equal. Suetin) **15...Qd7 16.f4?!** exf4 17.Bxf4 Nd5 18.Bg3 Bd6! 19.Bxd6 Qxd6 20.Ne4 Qc7** (20...Qf4 21.Rf1 Qe3+ 22.Kh1 Nf4?? 23.Rf3 wins. Suetin) **21.Qf3 Rad8** (21...Nf4!? 22.Nxf6+? gxf6 23.Qxc6 Nxh3+!. Suetin) **22.Rf1 Nde7!** (With the idea of Bd5; on 22...Ne5 23.Qg3 Ng6 24.Qxc7 Nxc7 25.d4 is equal. Suetin) **23.Rad1 Bd5 24.Qf2** (24.c4 Bxe4 25.Qxe4

Nd4) **24...f5! 25.gxf5** (25.Ng5!? Qd7! [25...fxg4? 26.Bxd5+ Nxd5 27.Qxf8+ Rxf8 28.Rxf8+ Kxf8 29.Ne6+ winning] 26.Qe2 fxg4! favors Black. Suetin) **25...Nxf5 26.Nc1 h6!** (26...Bxe4? 27.Bxe4 Ng3?? 28.Bd5+) **27.Qe1 Ne5 28.Rd2 Ng6! 29.Rdf2 Ngh4 30.Ne2** (30.Bh1 Bxe4 31.Bxe4 Qg3+) **30...Nxg2 31.Rxg2 Bxe4 32.dxe4 Ne3 33.Rxf8+ Rxf8 34.Rg3** (34.Rf2 Rd8!. Suetin) **34...Rf1+ 35.Qxf1 Nxf1 36.Kxf1 Qf7+ 37.Ke1 Qxa2 38.e5 Qb1+ 39.Kf2 Qf5+ 40.Rf3 Qxe5 White Resigns.**

Game 118
Arencibia-Kramnik
Biel 1993

   1.e4 c5 2.d3 Nc6 3.g3 d5 4.Nd2 Nf6 5.Bg2 e5 6.exd5 Nxd5 7.Ngf3 g6 8.0-0 Bg7 9.Nc4 0-0 10.Re1 Re8 11.Ng5 Rf8 12.c3 h6 13.Ne4 b6 14.a4 Be6 15.h4 Qe7 16.a5

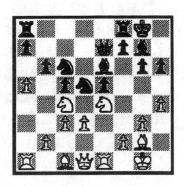

16...f5 17.Qa4 fxe4 18.Qxc6 Rac8 19.Qd6 Qf6 20.Rxe4 Rcd8 21.Qc6 Ne7 22.Qa4 Qxf2+ 23.Kh1 Qxg3 24.Be3 Nf5 25.Rg1 Nxh4 26.Nxe5 b5 White Resigns.

Game 119
Damljanovic-Kupreichik
Vidmar Memorial 1989

1.Nf3 d5 2.g3 c5 3.Bg2 Nc6 4.0-0 e5 5.d3 Nf6 6.Bg5 Be7 7.Nc3 d4

8.Bxf6 Bxf6 9.Ne4 Be7 10.c3 0-0 11.Qa4 Bd7 12.Rfc1 b6 13.Qd1 f5
14.Ned2 dxc3 15.bxc3 Rc8 16.Nc4 Qc7 17.Rab1 Rcd8 18.Qc2 Kh8
19.a4 Be6 20.Nfd2 Bg5 21.Rd1 Bxd2 22.Nxd2 Na5 23.c4 h6 24.Qb2
Bd7 25.Ra1 Bc6 26.f3 Qd7 27.Re1 Rfe8 28.Bh3 Kg8 29.Ra3 g6 30.e4
Bxa4 31.exf5 Bc6 32.Rxe5 Qd4+ 33.Qxd4 Rxd4 34.Rxe8+ Bxe8
35.Ne4 gxf5 36.Bxf5 Nc6 37.Nf6+ Kf8 38.Nxe8 Kxe8 39.Be4 Ne5
40.Rxa7 Nxd3 41.Rb7 Ne5 42.Rxb6 Nxc4 43.Rc6 Nd2 44.Rxc5 Nxe4
45.Re5+ Kf7 46.Rxe4 Rd2 47.h4 Kf6 48.Kf1 h5 49.Re2 Rd3 50.Kf2
Kf5 51.Re8 Ra3 52.Rg8 Ra2+ 53.Kg1 Ra1+ 54.Kg2 Ra2+ 55.Kh3
Black Resigns.

Game 120
Larsen-Ljubojevic
Manila 1974

1.Nf3 c5 2.g3 d5 3.Bg2 Nc6 4.0-0 e5 5.d3 Be7 6.e4 d4 7.a4

(see next diagram)

7...g5!? (Original, but not particularly effective if White responds correctly) **8.Nbd2 Be6 9.Nc4 f6 10.h4?!** (Correct was 10.Ne1 h5 11.f4 +=,

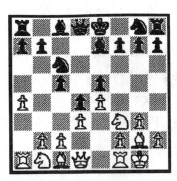

After 7.a4

by analogy to the Classical Variation of the King's Indian Defense) 10...h6 11.Nh2 gxh4 12.Qh5+ Kd7 13.Qxh4 f5 14.Qh5 Nf6 15.Qe2 fxe4 16.dxe4 Qg8 17.b3 h5 18.f4 Bxc4 19.Qxc4 Qxc4 20.bxc4 Rag8 21.fxe5 Nxe5 22.Bf4 Bd6 23.Rab1 Kc7 24.Nf3 Nxf3+ 25.Rxf3 Nxe4 26.Rfb3 b6 27.Bxd6+ Nxd6 28.Bd5 Rg5 29.Re1 Rh7 30.Kg2 Rhg7 31.Kh2 Nf5 32.a5 Ne3 33.axb6+ axb6 34.Ra1 Nxd5 35.cxd5 Kd6 36.Rxb6+ Kxd5 37.Ra3 h4 38.gxh4 Rg2+ 39.Kh3 Rg1 White Resigns.

Game 121
Stein-Zinn
Helsinki 1961

1.Nf3 d5 2.g3 c5 3.Bg2 Nc6 4.0-0 e5 5.d3 Be7 6.Nbd2 Nf6 7.e4 Bg4?!

8.h3 Be6 (8...Bh5 9.g4 Bg6 10.Nh4! +=) **9.Qe2 dxe4 10.dxe4 0-0 11.c3 Nd7 12.Nc4 b5 13.Ne3 c4 14.Rd1 Qc7 15.Nd5 Bxd5 16.exd5 Na5 17.Nd4! exd4 18.Qxe7 Rae8 19.Bf4! Qxf4 20.Qxd7! Qf6 21.Rxd4 Re2 22.Rf4 Qb6 23.b4 Nb7 24.a4 Nd6 25.axb5 Nxb5 26.Qc6 Rc2 27.Qxb6 axb6 28.Rxc4 Rxc3 29.Rc6 f5 30.Bf1 Rxc6 31.dxc6 Nd6 32.Rd1 Nc8 33.Bc4+ Kh8 34.c7 g6 35.Rd8 Kg7 36.Be6 Black Resigns.**

Game 122
Shirov-Bareev
Novgorod 1994

1.e4 c5 2.Nf3 e6 3.d3 d5 4.Nbd2 b6 5.g3 Nf6 6.c3 (The game Morozevich-Kogan, London 1994, continued 6.Bg2 dxe4?! 7.dxe4 Ba6 8.e5! – see next game for this) **6...Ba6** (Trying to inconvenience White along the a6-f1 diagonal, but White counters effectively) **7.c4 dxe4 8.dxe4 Bb7**

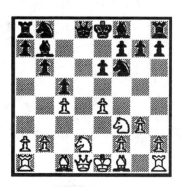

9.Bg2! Qc7 (On 9...Nxe4 10.Ng5! Nd6 [10...Qxg5 11.Nxe4 Qe7 12.Nd6+] 11.Bxb7 Nxb7 12.Nxf7! Kxf7 13.Qf3+ and 14.Qxb7 follows, while if 9...Bxe4 then 10.Nxe4 Qxd1+ 11.Kxd1 Nxe4 12.Ng5! Nxf2+ 13.Ke2 Nxh1 14.Bxa8 wins) **10.e5** (The "usual KIA central pawn thrust, but in a semi-open setting which gives rise to some interesting tactical possibilities) **10...Ng4 11.0-0!** Nc6 (Not 11...Nxe5? 12.Nxe5 Bxg2 13.Kxg2 Qxe5 14.Qf3 winning) **12.Ne4! Rd8** (On 12...Ngxe5 13.Nxe5 Nxe5 14.Bf4 gives White a tremendous initiative) **13.Qa4 Qd7** (After

13...Ngxe5 14.Nxe5 Qxe5 15.Bf4 Black gets roasted) **14.Bg5 Ncxe5??**
(An amazing blunder for a player rated 2675. He had to play 14...Nd4)
15.Rad1! (Now Black realizes his error, as 15...Qxa4 allows 16.Rxd8#!,
while if 15...Nd3 16.Rxd3) **Black Resigns.**

Game 123
Morozevich-A.Kogan
London 1994

**1.e4 c5 2.Nf3 e6 3.d3 d5 4.Nbd2 b6 5.g3 Nf6 6.Bg2 dxe4?! 7.dxe4
Ba6** (Trying to harass White along the a6-f1 diagonal, but this natural-
looking idea doesn't work out so well) **8.e5!** (A strong central reaction
to Black's "flank idea") **8...Nd5 9.c4!** (This looks awful as it weakens d3
and d4 and even drives Black's Knight toward the weakened squares.
But White has seen deeply into the following complications) **9...Nb4
10.0-0 Bb7** (Already Black must return the QB to meet threats along the
h1-a8 diagonal)

11.b3! N8c6 (On 11...Nd3 White continues 12.Ba3! with Qe2 and Rad1
to follow. This and other notes based on commentary by Morozevich)
12.Bb2 Qc7 13.a3! (He even invites the Knight to invade the "weak"
square) **13...Nd3 14.Bc3 0-0-0 15.Qe2** (Notice that the Nd3 is "surrounded." White threatens to bring his Rooks to the d-file and thus place
the errant Knight in real trouble) **15...Be7 16.Rfd1 Rd7 17.Nf1 Rhd8
18.Rd2!** (Threatening simply 19.Rad1 winning a piece) **18...f6?!** (A

better try was 18...Ndxe5!? though after 19.Nxe5 Nxe5 20.Bxe5 Rxd2 21.Nxd2 Rxd2 22.Bxb7+ Kxb7 23.Qxd2 Qxe5 24.Rd1! Qc7 [24...Bf6 25.Qd3!] 25.Qd3! White should win) **19.exf6 gxf6** (Or 19...Bxf6 20.Bxf6 gxf6 21.Qxe6) **20.Rad1!?** (Also strong was 20.Qxe6) **20...Nde5 21.Nxe5 fxe5 22.Rxd7 Rxd7 23.Rxd7 Kxd7** (Also after 23...Qxd7 24.Bxe5 White has a won game) **24.Bxe5!** (A neat shot; now 24...Qxe5?? loses to 25.Bxc6+) **24...Nxe5 25.Bxb7 Nxc4 26.bxc4 Qxb7 27.Qd3+ Ke8 28.Qxh7 b5** (Striving to get a passed pawn is the only way to continue to resist) **29.Qg6+ Kd7 30.Qd3+ Kc7 31.cxb5 Qd5 32.Qxd5 exd5 33.Ne3 c4** (On 33...Kd6 34.Nf5+ Ke6 35.Nxe7 Kxe7 36.h4 wins easily – White has an outside passer on both sides of the board) **34.Nxd5+ Kd7 35.Nxe7!** (The final point. Now after 35...Kxe7 36.Kf1 the White King gets in front of the enemy c-pawn; while 35...c3 36.Nc6! c2 37.Ne5+ and 38.Nd3 also wins handily) **Black Resigns.**

Game 124
Todorcevic-Yudasin
Las Palmas 1993

   1.e4 c5 2.d3 Nc6 3.g3 d5 4.Nd2 e6 5.Bg2 Nf6 6.Ngf3 Be7 7.0-0 b6 8.Re1 Bb7 9.c3 0-0 10.a4?!

(10.Qe2 with the idea of e5 was better. This and the following notes are based on commentary by Yudasin) **10...Qc7! 11.exd5** (11.Nf1 dxe4! 12.Bf4 [12.dxe4 Rad8 with the idea of Qc8-a8 is strong] 12...Qd8

13.dxe4 Qxd1 14.Raxd1 Rfd8 with a following Na5 is good for Black) **11...Nxd5 12.Nc4 Rad8 13.Qb3 Ba6! 14.Bg5 h6 15.Bxe7 Ndxe7 16.Qc2 Rd5! 17.a5!? b5 18.Ne3 Rd6?!** (18...Rd7! 19.Ng4! Ng6 20.h4 Rfd8 21.h5 Nge7 22.Nge5 Nxe5 23.Nxe5 Rd6 is unclear) **19.Nd2! b4** (19...Ne5 20.Ne4 Rdd8 21.Nxc5! Qxc5 22.d4 slightly favors White) **20.Nec4 Rd7 21.Ne4 Bxc4! 22.dxc4 Nxa5 23.Qa4! Nxc4 24.Nxc5 Rd2! 25.cxb4!** (25.Qxb4 Nxb2 26.c4 Rfd8 is strong for Black) **25...Nc8 26.Rac1! N8d6 27.b3 Nb6 28.Qa6 Qe7 29.Rcd1! Rxd1 30.Rxd1** (=) **30...Rb8 31.b5!** (With the idea of Bc6 +=) **31...Nd5 32.Bxd5 exd5 33.Qc6!** (33.Rxd5 Qe1+ 34.Kg2 Nxb5 =+) **33...Rxb5! 34.Rxd5 Rb6 35.Qa8+ Kh7 36.Rd1 g6 37.Qd5 Nf5 38.Qc4 Rc6 39.b4 h5 40.Qb3 Rc7 41.Qd3?!** (41.Qf3!? or 41.Qa2!?) **41...a5! 42.Na6 Rc6! 43.Qb5** (On 43.b5 Rd6 is strong, or 43.bxa5 Qb7!) **43...Rc2! 44.Qd3** (44.Qxa5 Qe2 45.Rf1 Ne3 wins, while 44.bxa5 Qf6! is strong) **44...Rb2 45.Qc3? Qe2! 46.Rf1 Rd2! 47.Nc5 axb4 48.Qf6 Kg8! 49.Nb3 Rd1 White Resigns.**

Game 125
Nadyrhanov-Saltaev
Tashkent 1993

1.e4 c5 2.Nf3 e6 3.d3 d5 4.Nbd2 Nf6 5.g3 b6 6.Bg2 Nc6 7.0-0 Be7 8.Re1 Bb7 9.c3 Qc7 10.e5 (10.Qe2) **10...Nd7 11.Nf1!?** (11.Qe2 g5! 12.g4 h5 13.h3 hxg4 14.hxg4 0-0-0 with the idea of Rag8. On 11.d4? cxd4 12.cxd4 Nb4! 13.Re3 Qc2! is strong)

11...Ncxe5?(Better 11...0-0-0) **12.Nxe5 Nxe5 13.Bf4 Bd6 14.Bxe5 Bxe5 15.Qh5 Bf6?** (15...Bd6 16.Rxe6+ Kf8 17.Re2 with White on top, e.g., 17...d4 18.cxd4 cxd4 19.Bxb7 Qxb7 20.Rc1 Rc8 21.Qd5!) **16.Rxe6+ Kf8 17.Rxf6! gxf6 18.Qh6+ Ke7** (18...Kg8 19.Ne3 followed by Ng4 will win) **19.Re1+ Kd7 20.Qxf6 Black Resigns.**

Game 126
Hracek-Zueger
Altensteig 1995

1.e4 e6 2.d3 d5 3.Nd2 Nf6 4.Ngf3 b6 5.g3 dxe4?! 6.dxe4 Bb7 7.Qe2 Nc6 8.c3 a5?! 9.Nc4?!

(Deserving attention was 9.Qb5! with the idea of Qa4 and Bb5) **9...Bc5 10.Bg5 h6 11.Rd1 Qe7 12.Bxf6 gxf6 13.Bg2 0-0 14.0-0 Rad8 15.e5 Ba6 16.exf6 Qxf6 17.Nfd2 Ne7 18.h4 Nf5 19.Ne4 Qg7 20.Nxc5 bxc5 21.Rxd8 Rxd8 22.Rc1 Nd6 23.b3 a4** (=) **24.Qd2 axb3 25.axb3 Bxc4 26.bxc4 Qf6 27.Qe2 Kg7 28.Qh5 Qf5 29.Qe2 Rb8 30.Bf1 Rb3 31.Qe3 Rb2 32.Bd3 Qh5 33.Ra1 Rb8 34.Kg2 Nf5 35.Qe5+ Kg8 36.Qxc7 Rf8 37.Ra5 Qg4 38.Bxf5 Qxf5 39.Qxc5 Qe4+ 40.Kh2 Rd8 41.Ra1 Rd2 42.Rc1 Kg7 43.Kg1 Rd3 44.Qc7 e5 45.c5 h5 46.Rf1 Rxc3 47.Qe7 Qf5 48.Qd6 Rd3 49.Qc7 Rd2 50.Qb6 Rc2 51.Qb1 Kg6 52.Qd1 Kg7 53.Qd5 Qf6 54.Kg2 Kg8 55.Qd1 Qf5 56.Qd6 Kg7 57.Kg1 Qf6 58.Qd5 Kg8 59.Qa8+ Kg7 60.Qa3 Qf5 61.Qe3 f6 62.Rc1 Qd7**

63.Kh2 Rxc1 64.Qxc1 Qc6 65.Qc3 Kf8 66.Qb4 Qf3 67.c6+ Ke8 68.Qc5 Kd8 69.Qd6+ Ke8 70.Qd7+ Kf8 71.Kg1 Black Resigns.

Game 127
Chuchelov-Dvoris
Cappelle la Grande

1.Nf3 Nf6 2.g3 c5 3.Bg2 Nc6 4.0-0 d5 5.d3 b6?! (Poorly timed) **6.c4! Bb7**

7.d4! e6 (7...dxc4 8.Ne5 Rc8 9.dxc5 Qxd1 10.Rxd1 bxc5 Na3 strongly favors White. Dvoris. Most of the following notes are based on Chuchelov's commentary) **8.Nc3 Rc8** (8...dxc4 9.Ne5 Nd5 10.Qa4 Rc8 11.Nxd5 exd5 12.e4! b5 [12...a6 13.exd5 b5 14.dxc6! bxa4 15.cxb7 wins.] 13.Qxb5 Qb6 14.Qxb6 axb6 15.exd5 Nxd4 16.d6! Ne2+ 17.Kh1 Bxg2+ 18.Kxg2 Bxd6 19.Nxc4 is powerful for White. Dvoris) **9.cxd5 Nxd5 10.e4 Nxc3 11.bxc3 cxd4 12.cxd4 Be7** (12...Ba6? is met by 13.d5! Bxf1 14.Bxf1 with a tremendous attack. Also, after 12...Nb4 13.d5 [also strong is 13.Ba3] 13...exd5 14.exd5 Qxd5 15.Re1+ Be7 16.Ba3 White again has a terrific attacking game) **13.d5 Na5 14.Qa4+ Kf8 15.Ne5 exd5 16.exd5 f6 17.Nc6 Qd7 18.Ba3** (18.Rd1! Nxc6 19.dxc6 Bxc6 20.Rxd7 Bxa4 21.Rxa7. Dvoris) **18...Nxc6 19.dxc6 Bxc6 20.Bxe7+ Kxe7 21.Rfe1+ Kf7 22.Qb3+ Kg6 23.Rad1 Qb7 24.Qd3+ Kh6** (24...Kf7 25.Qc4+ is strong) **25.Qe3+ Kg6 26.Bf1! Rhe8 27.Bd3+ Kf7 28.Bc4+ Kf8?** (28...Kg6 29.Qf4! h6 [29...Bh1 30.Qg4+ Kh6 31.Qh3+

Kg6 32.g4 h6 33.Qd3+ Be4 34.Rxe4 wins] 30.Be6!? with the idea 30...Rxe6 31.Rxe6 Bh1 32.Rxf6+! Kh7 [32...gxf6 33.Qg4+ Kf7 34.Rd7+ Ke8 35.Qe6+ winning] 33.Qf5+ Kg8 34.Qe6+ Kh8 35.f3 wins) **29.Qa3+ Re7 30.Ba6 Black Resigns.**

Game 128
Rivas Pastor-Illescas
Cordoba Spain 1993

   1.g3 e5 2.Bg2 d5 (Note we have a Modern Defense with colors reversed. We believe it gives White good chances for an initiative due to the extra tempo) **3.d3 c5?!** (Too ambitious. The more restrained 3...Nf6 [or 3...Nc6] or the solid 3...c6 would be wiser) **4.e4! Nf6** (The ending after 4...dxe4 5.dxe4 Qxd1+ 6.Kxd1 would slightly favor White due to the hole on d5) **5.Nc3!** (Consistently attacking d5, which was weakened by 3...c5?!) **5...d4 6.Nce2 Nc6 7.f4**

(In effect White has a superior form of the KIA against a Reversed Classical System, since he has obtained the f4 break without the investment of time required after an early Ng1-f3 [a later move of the Nf3 to h4, e1, or perhaps d2 to achieve f2-f4 signifies this tempo investment] seen in the more traditional move orders of the KIA) **7...Bd6 8.Nf3 0-0 9.0-0 Bd7 10.Kh1** (10.f5 c4! 11.h3 [11.dxc4 Nxe4 is unclear] 11...Rc8 12.g4 cxd3 13.cxd3 Nb4 14.Ne1 Qc7 15.Bd2 Bb5! is good for Black. Illescas. Most of the remaining notes are from Illescas' commentary)

10...Rc8 11.c3! (11.f5 c4!) **11...dxc3 12.bxc3 Bg4! 13.d4?** (Correct was 13.h3 Bxf3 14.Bxf3 b5, or 13.Rb1 with an edge to White in either case) **13...cxd4 14.cxd4 Nxe4 15.fxe5** (15.dxe5 Bc5 16.Qxd8 Rfxd8 17.h3 Be6 is strong for Black) **15...Be7 16.Be3** (16.d5? Bc5! 17.Qb3?! Nxe5! 18.Nxe5 Bxe2) **16...Nb4** (=+; White's center is fixed and the d5 square beckons to Black's pieces) **17.Bg1 Qd7!?** (17...Nd5) **18.Nf4! Nc3 19.Qd2 Ncd5 20.Ne1!? Bg5! 21.a3 Nc6 22.Ned3 b6 23.Qa2** (23.Bxd5 Qxd5 -+) **23...Nc3! 24.Qf2 Bxf4 25.Nxf4 Ne7! 26.h3 Be6 27.g4 Ncd5 28.Nh5?** (Better 28.Nxe6 fxe6 +=) **28...Rc3 29.Qd2 Rfc8 30.Rf3?! Rc2 31.Qg5?** (31.Qd3) **31...Ng6 32.Nxg7 Kxg7 33.Raf1 Qe7 34.Rf6 h6 35.Qh5 Rxg2! 36.Kxg2 Qb7 37.Kg3** (37.Kh2 Rc2+ 38.Rf2 Rxf2+ 39.Rxf2 Ndf4 wins) **37...Rc3+ 38.R1f3** (38.Kh2 Nxf6 39.exf6+ Kh7 wins) **38...Ndf4! 39.Rxc3** and **White Resigned** (as 39...Qg2 is mate).

Game 129
Todorcevic-Illescas
Cordoba Spain 1992

1.g3 e5 2.Bg2 d5 3.d3 Nc6 4.Nf3 f5

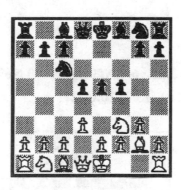

(Aiming for a Reversed Austrian Attack vs. a Reversed Pirc – or if you like, simply a KIA. But again, White's extra tempo must give him good play) **5.0-0 Nf6 6.a3?!** (We like the thematic central blow 6.c4! with a slight edge for White. Most of the remaining notes based on commentary of Illescas) **6...Bd6 7.b4 e4! 8.Ne1?!** (8.Nfd2 h5!) **8...Be6!** (8...h5 9.c4)

9.Bb2 Qe7 10.c4!? dxc4 11.dxe4 fxe4! 12.Nc2 0-0-0 (-+) 13.Qe1! h5? (13...Kb8) **14.b5! Ne5 15.Qa5! h4!? 16.Bxe5! Bxe5 17.b6 axb6** (17...hxg3 18.bxa7!) **18.Qxe5 hxg3! 19.Nc3** (19.hxg3 Rd5 20.Qc3 [20.Qf4 g5 wins] 20...Qf7 is winning for Black. Also on 19.Nd4 Black plays 19...Ng4!! as 20.Qxe6+ Qxe6 21.Nxe6 gxh2+ 22.Kh1 Rd1! is decisive; or if 20.Qxe4 then 20...Rxd4! 21.Qxd4 Qh4 22.h3 gxf2+ 23.Kh1 Qg3 wins. Furthermore, if 19.Qxg3 then 19...Nh5! 20.Qe3 [20.Qe5 Rd5! 21.Qxe4 Nf6 is very strong for Black] 20...Bf5 with ideas of 21...Qh4 and ...Nf4 is very threatening. However, to be considered was 19.fxg3 and on 19...Rxh2 20.Ne3! with murky play) **19...Rxh2! 20.Qxg3** (20.Nxe4?? Rxg2+ wins) **20...Rdh8 21.Ne3** (21.Qxh2? Rxh2 22.Kxh2 Ng4+ wins for Black) **21...Qc5! 22.Rac1 R2h5!?** (22...Qh5 23.f3!) **23.Rfd1 Rg5 24.Qf4 Bh3! 25.Ncd5?** (Correct was 25.Nxe4! with ongoing complications) **25...Rxg2+! 26.Nxg2 Nxd5 27.Qxe4 Bxg2! 28.Qxg2 Nf6! 29.Rc3 Kb8 30.Rh3 Rf8! 31.Qxg7 Ne4 32.e3 Qf5 33.f3 Ka7! 34.Rf1** (Or 34.fxe4 Qxh3 35.Qxf8 Qg4+ winning) **34...Qxh3 35.Qxf8 Ng3 White Resigns.**

Game 130
Gufeld-Hodgson
Calcutta 1993

1.g3 d5 2.Bg2 e5 3.d3 g6 4.Nf3 Bg7 5.0-0 Ne7 6.e4 0-0 7.Nbd2 h6 8.c3 Nbc6 9.Re1 Be6 (9...Re8) **10.Qc2?!**

(Better 10.exd5!? and if 10...Nxd5 11.Nc4 +=; or if 10...Bxd5 11.Qe2) **10...a5 11.b3 g5!? 12.Ba3 Re8 13.exd5 Nxd5 14.Nc4** (Now this is not so strong) **14...Nxc3! 15.Ncxe5** (15.Qxc3 e4 16.Nfe5 Bxc4 17.Qxc4 Nxe5 [17...Bxe5?! 18.Rad1 exd3 19.Rxd3 Qf6 20.Rf3! Qe6 21.Qxe6 Rxe6 22.Rfe3] 18.Qxe4 Nxd3 19.Qxe8+ Qxe8 20.Rxe8+ Rxe8 21.Rd1 Nb4 22.Bxb7 Nxa2 23.Rd7 – this and the following commentary based on Gufeld's analysis) **15...Nb5 16.Bb2 Nb4 17.Qd2 g4!?** (=) **18.Nxg4?** (18.Nh4 Qg5) **18...Bxg4 19.Rxe8+ Qxe8 20.Bxg7 Kxg7 21.Re1 Be6! 22.Ne5 c6! 23.Ng4?! Bxg4 24.Rxe8 Rxe8 25.h3 Bf5! 26.g4 Bg6 27.f4 f6 28.f5?** (Better tries were 28.g5!? or 28.h4!?) **28...Bf7 29.h4 Nd4 30.g5 Nd5 31.Qf2 Ne2+ 32.Kh2 hxg5 33.hxg5 Rh8+ White Resigns.**

Game 131
Ljubojevic-Karpov
Linares 1992

1.e4 c6 2.d3 d5 (The Caro-Kann Defense against the KIA. One advantage of this move order is that two important defensive systems – the London System and the Keres System are circumvented. That is, the characteristic ...Bf5 of the London System [see Game 134] is impossible, while the move ...Bg4 – essential to the Keres System – is discouraged) **3.Nd2 e5** (The most natural move. Black can try to insist on ...Bg4 by 3...dxe4 4.dxe4 Nf6 5.Ngf3 Bg4, but White will retain an edge after simply 6.h3 – see the game L.Stein-I.Birbrager given in the introduction) **4.Ngf3 Bd6 5.Qe2!?**

(see next diagram)

5...Nf6 (For 5...Qe7 see the next game) **6.g3** (Sharper is 6.d4!? dxe4 7.Nxe5 Bf5 8.h3 h5, e.g., 9.Ndc4! Be7 10.Bd2! Nbd7 11.0-0-0 Nb6 [so far Timman-Seirawan, Cannes 1992] and now instead of the actually played 12.Ne3!? Be6 13.Ba5? Bxa2!, Seirawan gives 12.Ba5 with a clear advantage for White. The rest of the notes are mainly based on commentary by Karpov) **6...0-0 7.Bg2 Re8 8.0-0 a5! 9.a3** (9.a4 Na6) **9...a4** (=+)

After 5.Qe2!?

10.b4 axb3e.p. 11.cxb3 Bg4 12.Bb2 Nbd7 13.h3 Bh5 14.Qe3 d4 (More accurate was 14...Qe7! and on 15.b4 d4 16.Qe1 Bxf3! 17.Bxf3 b5 followed by c5 with a clear positional advantage for Black) **15.Qe1 b5 16.Qc1 Ra6 17.Qc2 Bxf3 18.Bxf3 Qb6 19.Rfc1 Rea8 20.Nb1 Qd8** (To be considered was 20...h5 21.h4 g6 22.Bd1 Bf8 and ...Bh6 with an edge for Black) **21.Bd1** (The passiveness of White's position, due mainly to the anemic a-pawn, is the basis for Black's positional edge) **21...Nf8 22.Qe2 Qe7 23.Kg2 Ne6 24.Rc2 Nc5 25.Nd2 Ne6 26.Nb1 h5** (Black maneuvers to increase the pressure on White's position) **27.h4 g6 28.Bc1 Qd7 29.Rca2 Ng4 30.Qc2 Be7 31.Bf3 Kg7 32.a4 Nf6 33.Bd2 Nc5 34.Be1** (Not 34.Bb4?? Nxd3) **34...Qe6 35.Nd2 R6a7 36.Be2 Na6! 37.Nf3 Nb4 38.Bxb4 Bxb4** (Enhancing control of the dark squares and thus maintaining the edge) **39.Ng5 Qd7 40.axb5 Rxa2 41.Rxa2 Rxa2 42.Qxa2 cxb5 43.Qa6 Ne8 44.Nf3 f6 45.Ng1 Nd6 46.Qb6?!** (46.Nh3 Qb7 47.Qa2) **46...Qb7!** (=+) **47.Qd8?** (47.Qxb7 =+) **47...Nf7 48.Qe8?** (48.Qd5 -+) **48...Be7!** (Suddenly White's Queen is threatened by 48...Nd6 and there is no remedy) **49.Bxh5** (Utter desperation) **49...gxh5 50.Nh3 f5 51.f3 fxe4 52.fxe4 b4 53.Nf2 Qc7 54.Kf1 Qd6 55.Kg2 Bd8 56.Nh3 Qg6 57.Kh2 Qg4 58.Qb5 Qe2+ 59.Kg1 Qd1+ 60.Kg2 Qxb3 White Resigns.**

Game 132
Anand-Karpov
Brussels 1991 (1st match game)

1.e4 c6 2.d3 d5 3.Nd2 e5 4.Ngf3 Bd6 5.Qe2!? Qe7

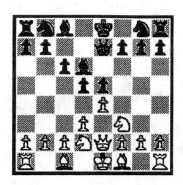

(On 5...Nd7 6.exd5 cxd5 7.Nxe5 Nxe5 8.d4 [8.f4?! Bg4] 8...Qe7 9.dxe5 Qxe5 10.Nf3 +=. This and most of the following notes based on Karpov's commentary) **6.d4 exd4 7.exd5 cxd5 8.Nxd4 Nc6 9.N2b3 Nf6** (Interesting would be 9...Nxd4 10.Nxd4 Be5 with unclear play) **10.Qxe7+!** (The ending will be slightly in White's favor mainly due to the isolani) **10...Kxe7 11.Bd2 Re8 12.0-0-0 a6 13.f3** (A standard move in such positions, controlling e4 and allowing the possibility of a later space gaining advance with g4) **13...Kf8 14.Bc3 Ne5 15.Kb1 b6 16.Bd3 Nxd3 17.Rxd3 Bd7 18.Rdd1 Rac8 19.Nc1 Nh5** (19...Ng8!? with the idea of f6, Kf7 and Ne7 is equal. Karpov) **20.g3 g6 21.Nd3** (Threatening 22.Nb4) **21...a5 22.Bd2 f6 23.Rhe1 Rxe1 24.Bxe1** (24.Rxe1 Kf7 =) **24...Ng7** (Now 24...Kf7 is met by 25.g4 and Bg3 +=) **25.Bf2 Bc7 26.b4!? Kf7 27.b5 Nf5 28.a4** (On 28.Nxf5 Bxf5 29.Nb2? Bxc2+ 30.Kxc2 Bxg3+ wins) **28...Ne7 29.Ne2 g5** (=) **30.g4 Ng6 31.h3 Be6 32.Nd4 Bd7 33.Rh1?! Rh8! 34.Rc1** (Better was 34.h4 h5 35.hxg5 hxg4 36.Rxh8 Nxh8 37.fxg4 Bxg4 38.gxf6 =) **34...Ne5! 35.Nxe5 fxe5 36.Ne2 h5 37.Nc3 Be6 38.Rd1 hxg4 39.hxg4 Rd8 40.Be3 Kg6 41.Bc1 Rd7 42.Bb2 d4 43.Ne4 Rf7 44.Bc1 Bd8 45.Rh1 Rxf3 46.Rh8 Bf6 47.Nxf6**

Rxf6 48.Rd8 Bxg4 49.Rg8+ Kf7 50.Rxg5 Bf5 51.Rh5 e4 52.Bb2 Kg6 53.Rh1 Rd6 54.Rd1 d3 55.cxd3 e3! 56.Be5 Re6 57.Bd4 e2 58.Re1 Bxd3+ 59.Kb2 Bf5? (Time pressure. Correct was 59...Kf5 60.Kc3 Ke4 with good winning chances) **60.Bxb6!** (This resource saves the day for White) **60...Rxb6 61.Rxe2 Rd6 62.Kc3! Rd3+ 63.Kc4 Ra3 64.Kc5 Rxa4 65.b6 Rb4 66.Ra2 Rb1 67.Rxa5 Be4** (Playing on out of sheer momentum, as the game is definitely drawn) **68.Rb5 Rc1+ 69.Kd6 Bb7 70.Rc5 Rb1 71.Kc7 Bh1 72.Rc6+ Bxc6 73.Kxc6 Kf7 74.b7 Ke7 75.Kc7 Rc1+ 76.Kb6 Draw.**

Game 133
Balashov-Groszpeter
Dortmund 1992

   1.e4 c6 2.d3 d5 3.Nd2 e5 4.Ngf3 Bd6 5.g3 Nf6 6.Bg2 0-0 7.0-0 Re8 8.b3

(A novel approach. The most usual move is 8.Re1) **8...Bg4?! 9.h3 Bxf3?!** (Giving up the two Bishops allows White a small but persistent positional plus. After the more circumspect 9...Bh5 we still like White's chances – see Games 51- 53 for this type of play, via the Keres System move order) **10.Qxf3 Nbd7** (On 10...Bb4 11.Nb1! [preventing ...Bc3 and intending a2-a3 to repel the invader] is best; if 10...Qa5 [aiming for ...Ba3] then 11.a3 Qc3? 12.Ra2. These notes and most of the rest are based on commentary by Balashov) **11.Qe2 Qa5 12.a3 Qa6 13.Re1**

dxe4 14.Nxe4!? (Also good for a slight edge was 14.dxe4 Qxe2 15.Rxe2) **14...Nxe4 15.Qxe4 Bc5 16.Bb2 Qb6 17.Qe2** (After 17.Qf5? Balashov gives 17...Bd4! 18.c3 g6! 19.Qxd7 Bxf2+ 20.Kf1 [20.Kh2? Bxe1 21.Rxe1 Qf2 22.Rb1 Qc2 wins] 20...Bxe1 21.Rxe1 Rad8 22.Qg4 Rxd3 with very strong play for Black) **17...a5?** (Better was 17...Qd8!? +=. After 17...Re6?! 18.b4 Bf8 19.h4 [threatening Bh3] is strong. Or 17...Re7 18.b4 Bd6 19.c4 with clear advantage for White. Balashov) **18.d4!** (A nice tactical shot. Now 18...Bd6 19.d5 is good for White, as is 18...Bxd4 19.Bxd4 exd4 20.Qxe8+ Rxe8+ 21.Rxe8+ Nf8 22.Be4) **18...exd4 19.Qxe8+ Rxe8 20.Rxe8+ Nf8** (20...Bf8 21.Rd1 is powerful for White) **21.Rd1 h5 22.h4 Qc7 23.b4! axb4?** (The only way to resist was 23...Qb6, though Balashov's intended 24.c3! would be hard to meet) **24.axb4 Qb6 25.Ba3 Bxb4** (Or 25...Qa6 26.Rd3, and if 25...Bd6 26.c4) **26.Rb1 c5 27.Bxb4 cxb4 28.Ra1 g6 29.Raa8 d3 30.Rxf8+ Kg7 31.Bd5** (Threatening 32.Rxf7+ Kh6 33.Rh8#) **31...Kf6 32.Rae8 g5 33.Rxf7+** (Mate is forced after 33...Kg6 34.Rg8+ Kh6 35.hxg5#) **Black Resigns.**

Game 134
E.Pigusov-E.Sveshnikov
St.Petersburg 1993

1.Nf3 d5 2.g3 Nf6 3.Bg2 c6 4.0-0 Bf5 5.b3 e6 6.Bb2 Bd6

(A new but dubious plan. The usual 6...Be7 is preferable) **7.d3 0-0** (Sveshnikov gives 7...Qe7 8.Nbd2 Ba3 9.Qc1 [9.Bxa3 Qxa3] 9...Bxb2

10.Qxb2 0-0 with equality, but better is 8.a3 followed by 9.Nbd2, Qe1 and e4 with a slight edge for White) **8.Nbd2 Qe7 9.e4!? dxe4 10.dxe4 Nxe4** (10...Bxe4? 11.Bxf6 Bxf3 12.Bxe7 Bxd1 13.Bxf8 wins. This and most of the remaining notes are based on commentary of Sveshnikov) **11.Nd4!? Nxd2 12.Nxf5 exf5 13.Qxd2 Be5!?** (Better than 13...Ba3 14.Rfe1 Qd6 15.Qxd6! Bxd6 16.Rad1 Bb4 17.c3. Sveshnikov) **14.Bxe5** (14.Rfe1 f6! [14...Nd7? 15.Bxe5 Nxe5 16.Qc3. Sveshnikov] 15.Qe3 Qc7 16.Bxe5 fxe5 17.Qxe5 Qxe5 18.Rxe5 Nd7 19.Re7 Rf7 =) **14...Qxe5 15.Rfe1 Qc5 16.b4 Qb6 17.Rab1! a5?** (17...Na6 18.c4 Rad8 19.Qc2 Qd4!) **18.bxa5 Qxa5 19.Qxa5 Rxa5 20.Rxb7 Rxa2 21.Bf1! c5?** (Not 21...Rxc2?? 22.Reb1; but best was 21...Na6 22.Bc4 Ra4 23.Bb3 Nc5! [23...Rb4? 24.Rxf7 Nc5 25.Ree7!] 24.Bxa4 Nxb7 25.Bxc6 Nd6. Sves-nikov) **22.Bb5! Rb2** (22...Rxc2 23.Re8! Rxe8 24.Bxe8 Na6 25.Bb5 wins) **23.c4 Ra2 24.Be8 Ra8 25.Ree7 Kh8! 26.h4 g6 27.Kg2!** (Not 27.Bxf7? Nc6 28.Red7 Nd8 =) **27...Na6 28.Bxf7 Rab8** (28...Rfb8 29.Bd5 Rxb7 30.Bxb7 Ra7 31.Kf3 with the idea Kf4-g5-h6 winning) **29.h5?** (29.Ra7 Ra8 30.Bxg6! Rxa7 31.Rxa7 hxg6 32.Rxa6 Kg7 33.Rc6 wins) **29...Rxb7 30.Rxb7 gxh5 31.Bxh5 f4 32.g4 Nb4 33.Bf7 Kg7! 34.Bd5+ Kf6 35.Rxh7?** (Correct was 35.Be4) **35...Nxd5 36.cxd5 Ke5 37.Kf3 Kxd5 38.g5 Ke5 39.Kg4 f3 40.Re7+ Kd4! 41.g6 c4 42.g7 Rg8 43.Kxf3 Kd5 44.Ke3 Kd6 45.Ra7 Ke5!** (=) **46.Kd2 Kf6 47.Kc3 Rxg7** (After 48.Rxg7 Kxg7 49.Kxc4 Kf6 50.Kd4 Kf5 51.Ke3 Ke5 52.Kf3 Kf5 draws easily) **Draw.**